Teachers as Course Developers

CAMBRIDGE LANGUAGE EDUCATION
Series Editor: Jack C. Richards

This series draws on the best available research, theory, and educational practice to help clarify issues and resolve problems in language teaching, language teacher education, and related areas. Books in the series focus on a wide range of issues and are written in a style that is accessible to classroom teachers, teachers-in-training, and teacher educators.

In this series:

Agendas for Second Language Literacy *by Sandra Lee McKay*

Reflective Teaching in Second Language Classrooms *by Jack C. Richards and Charles Lockhart*

Educating Second Language Children: The whole child, the whole curriculum, the whole community *edited by Fred Genesee*

Understanding Communication in Second Language Classrooms *by Karen E. Johnson*

The Self-directed Teacher: Managing the learning process *by David Nunan and Clarice Lamb*

Functional English Grammar: An introduction for second language teachers *by Graham Lock*

Teachers as Course Developers *edited by Kathleen Graves*

Classroom-based Evaluation in Second Language Education *by Fred Genesee and John A. Upshur*

From Reader to Reading Teacher: Issues and strategies for second language classrooms *by Jo Ann Aebersold and Mary Lee Field*

Extensive Reading in the Second Language Classroom *by Richard R. Day and Julian Bamford*

Language Teaching Awareness: A guide to exploring beliefs and practices *by Jerry G. Gebhard and Robert Oprandy*

Teachers as Course Developers

Edited by

Kathleen Graves
School for International Training

Based on the accounts of Maria del Carmen Blyth,
Pat Fisher, Maria Estela Pinheiro Franco,
Barbara Fujiwara, Laura Hull, and Johan Uvin

CAMBRIDGE
UNIVERSITY PRESS

PUBLISHED BY THE PRESS SYNDICATE OF THE UNIVERSITY OF CAMBRIDGE
The Pitt Building, Trumpington Street, Cambridge, United Kingdom

CAMBRIDGE UNIVERSITY PRESS
The Edinburgh Building, Cambridge CB2 2RU, UK   http://www.cup.cam.ac.uk
40 West 20th Street, New York, NY 10011–4211, USA   http://www.cup.org
10 Stamford Road, Oakleigh, Melbourne 3166, Australia
Ruiz de Alarcón 13, 28014 Madrid, Spain

© Cambridge University Press 1996

First Published 1996
Fourth printing 1999

Printed in the United States of America

Library of Congress Cataloging-in-Publication Data
Teachers as course developers / edited by Kathleen Graves.
p.   cm. — (Cambridge language education)
Includes bibliographical references and index.
ISBN 0-521-49722-1 (hardback). — ISBN 0-521-49768-X (pbk.)
1. English language — Study and teaching — Foreign speakers —
Curricula. 2. English language — Teacher training. 3. English
teachers. I. Graves, Kathleen. II. Series
PE1128.T3567   1996
428′.007 — dc20   95-829
                                                          CIP

A catalog record for this book is available from the British Library.

ISBN 0 521 49722 1 hardback
ISBN 0 521 49768 X paperback

Contents

Contributors

Maria del Carmen Blyth, International School of Tanganyika, Dar Es
    Salaam, Tanzania
Pat Fisher, Canadian Academy, Kobe, Japan
Maria Estela Pinheiro Franco, Associação Alumni, São Paulo, Brazil
Barbara Fujiwara, Doshisha Women's Junior College, Kyoto, Japan
Kathleen Graves, School for International Training, Brattleboro, Vermont
Laura Hull, University of Washington
Johan Uvin, Massachusetts Department of Education

Series editor's preface

Teachers as Course Developers presents an insider's view of what course development involves. The contributors are classroom teachers, and each presents a different though complementary story about the kinds of problems faced in designing a course and how those problems can be solved.

Graves uses a framework of course design processes in setting the schema for the book and effectively uses that framework to show how these teachers responded to specific issues in course design and the kind of decision making they used to resolve problems. What is likely to be of most interest to readers, therefore, is not the specific solutions described or the details of the particular course developed, but the information the contributors give about framing the problem they faced, posing questions, gathering information and resources, and drawing on theory and experience, as well as the processes of syllabus development, teaching, and evaluation they used. The teachers' stories emphasize that course design is not necessarily the orderly linear process which is often described in textbooks of curriculum theory. Different teachers begin the process of curriculum development from various starting points, problematize their task in different ways, and use different strategies to achieve their goals.

Teachers and teacher educators will therefore find this book to be a valuable complement to existing texts on course design in language teaching. It presents a personal view of course design and illustrates the kind of thinking and planning teachers use – thinking which often goes unreported but which is a crucial dimension of teaching. Such thinking involves the teachers' personal values and experience, their beliefs and knowledge, as well as their interactions with colleagues and students in the contexts where they work. Like other titles in this series, *Teachers as Course Developers* aims to broaden our understanding of language teaching through an examination of the processes of second language teaching. Thus, teachers and teacher educators will find this book to be a source of rich and interesting data for analysis and discussion of curriculum design in language teaching.

Jack C. Richards

Preface

Teachers as Course Developers is designed to help teachers understand how to develop courses or modify existing ones using their own experiences as well as the experiences and theories of others. It attempts to capture that process in action through the stories of six teachers who, themselves, have developed courses.

Chapter 1 discusses teachers as course developers in a general sense. Chapter 2 describes a framework of components in course development – assessing needs; determining goals and objectives; conceptualizing content; deciding on materials, activities, and techniques; organizing content and activities; evaluating; and considering resources and constraints – as well as issues for teachers to consider in the process. Chapters 3 through 8 are the accounts of six experienced teachers who describe the process of developing a course. Each account is followed by an analysis and a set of questions and tasks that ask the reader to consider a particular aspect of the framework discussed in Chapter 2. A list of suggested readings appears at the end of the book for those interested in learning more about curriculum theory and course design processes.

Kathleen Graves

Acknowledgments

This book is the result of collaboration and discussion among many teachers. Its main purpose is to give teachers' voices and experiences a central place in the literature on second language curriculum design. Thus the heart of the book is the stories of the six teachers who describe the ins and outs and ups and downs of developing a course.

Other teachers also contributed during the field-testing of the material. Thanks to the thirty teachers who first used the material in my course design class at the School for International Training, and a special thanks to my "focus group" – Sistie Moffit, Jeanie Levesque, Beth Edwards, Holly Hahn, Joe Krupp, and Carolyn Layzer – for their suggestions and enthusiasm.

Steve Cornwell, Susan Pomeroy, and Suzanne Meyer read the manuscript and offered helpful comments at various stages in its development. Lise Minovitz lent a deft hand in editing portions of the text. Stacia Houston and Helen Smith helped with the mindmaps. My colleague Pat Moran provided me with the word *problematizing,* and Lesley Koustaff helped me see the importance of it.

I would also like to thank my two anonymous reviewers and Jack Richards, series editor, who synthesized the reviewers' suggestions into a coherent plan of action.

Thanks to the editorial staff at Cambridge University Press – Bonnie Biller, Sue André, Mary Carson, and Mary Vaughn – for their editorial expertise and support.

Finally, thanks to Donald Freeman for reading between and beyond the lines.

1 Teachers as course developers

Kathleen Graves

Purpose of this book

One afternoon, a teacher came into my office to discuss an independent study. "I have been asked to design an evening English course for adults in my town in Nicaragua." He paused and then continued, "I've never developed a course before. Are there any guidelines? Is there a procedure to follow? Where do I start?" I realized as I listened to him that I had heard these questions many times before, from many teachers, the difference being the nature of each teacher's situation. For example, one teacher explained that her school needed a course for the preteens who had finished their children's course but were too young for the teen course. Another teacher said, "I'm given some books and then told I can teach any way I want." A fourth teacher explained, "My students are in danger of losing their first language literacy. How do I design a course that enables them to maintain literacy in both languages?" The situations were different, but the questions were the same: Are there any guidelines? What do I do? Where do I start?

These teachers' situations are not unusual, as teachers are increasingly being called upon to design the courses they teach (Breen 1987; Nunan 1987; Richards 1990; Yalden 1987). The challenge for me, as a teacher educator, was both to help these teachers draw on their own experience to answer those questions and to provide them with a conceptual framework for making sense of the course development process. This book is an attempt to meet the challenge from those two perspectives. First, it will help teachers see that they do have experience in course development and recognize how that experience can serve as a basis for developing new courses or modifying existing ones. Second, the book will describe a framework of the components of course development that can help teachers make sense of a complex process. Thus the purpose of this book is to lead teachers to an understanding of how to develop courses from their own experience as well as from the experiences and theories of others. It attempts to capture that process in action through the stories of six teachers, each of whom developed a course.

Premises of the book

Helping teachers understand how to make use of their own experience as well as the theories of others raises questions about the relationship between theory and practice, which is a fundamental question for teachers and teacher educators. A distinction between theory in the general sense and theory in the personal sense may be useful. Prabhu (1990) defines theory in the general sense as an abstraction that attempts to unite diverse and complex phenomena into a single principle or system of principles so as to make sense of the phenomena. Personal theory, by contrast, is a subjective understanding of one's practice or "sense of plausibility" that provides coherence and direction for the teacher. Both the efforts of others to provide models and the teacher's own experience and understanding of that experience are part of how teachers make sense of what they do. In the words of Mary Kennedy (1991: 2), "Teachers, like other learners, interpret new content through their existing understandings and modify and reinterpret new ideas on the basis of what they already know or believe." Thus one premise of this book is that teachers develop and change from the inside out, through individual practice and reflection, and from the outside in, through contact with the experiences and theories of others.[1]

Another premise is that course development is a grounded process because it is about a specific course in a given time and place with a given set of people. It is not an orderly sequence of events but rather a complex, unpredictable, and individual process. The teacher herself is the most important variable in the process. A teacher develops a course in ways that reflect her experience and the values and priorities that are products of her experience as well as the prevailing wisdom around her. The more aware a teacher is of her values and priorities, the greater her understanding of why certain things make sense to her and the greater her ability to understand and resolve the dilemmas she will confront.

Contents of the book

This book is about teachers as course developers in two senses. It is about teachers such as the ones who asked the questions in the opening paragraph,

1 For a model of how teachers construct their understanding of their practice, see Colton and Sparks-Langer (1993).

and thus all teachers who are asking the same kinds of questions. Chapter 1 discusses teachers as course developers in this general sense. Chapter 2 describes a framework of components in course development and issues for the teacher to consider in the process. The book is also about course developers in a specific sense: the accounts of six experienced teachers who describe the process of developing a course in Chapters 3 through 8. Each account is followed by an analysis and a set of questions that ask the reader to consider a particular aspect of the framework discussed in Chapter 2. An annotated bibliography at the end of the book is intended for readers interested in learning more about curriculum theory and course design processes.

Course, curriculum, and syllabus

The terms *course, curriculum,* and *syllabus* have been assigned meanings by their users that often overlap. For example, Nunan (1987) discusses three ways in which the notion of curriculum has been interpreted by teachers: as a product or set of items to be taught, as a process for deriving materials and methodology, and as the planning (as opposed to the implementation or evaluation) phase of a program. For the purposes of this book, a curriculum will be understood in the broadest sense as the philosophy, purposes, design, and implementation of a whole program. A syllabus will be defined narrowly as the specification and ordering of content of a course or courses (White 1988). Hutchinson and Waters (1987:65) have defined a course as "an integrated series of teaching-learning experiences, whose ultimate aim is to lead the learners to a particular state of knowledge." Thus syllabus design is a part of course development, and a course is part of a curriculum. However, such strict definitions do not apply in practice, as some teachers may refer to the "curriculum" for their course and others to the "syllabus" for the curriculum. The distinction between a curriculum and a course is nevertheless important because some of the areas of concern in curriculum development may be out of the hands of teachers who are developing courses – for example, societal needs analysis, testing for placement purposes, or programwide evaluation.

In a broad sense, the process of course development is similar to that of curriculum development. Course development includes planning a course, teaching it, and modifying the plan, both while the course is in progress and after the course is over. In the traditional view of curriculum development, which Johnson (1989) calls a "specialist approach," teachers have no role in the planning stages, and specialists determine the purposes, plan the syllabus, and develop the materials that teachers are then supposed to use in

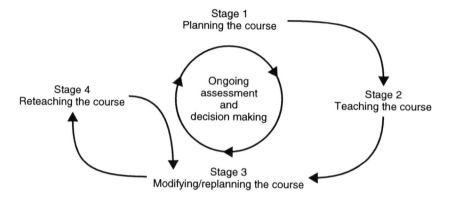

Figure 1   The process of course development for the teacher

their classrooms. Nevertheless, teachers who have never planned a new course still have experience in course development. This is because course development is more than just planning a course; it also includes teaching it, an experience that teachers, by definition, have. Furthermore, most courses also entail modification of the course, both while it is in progress and after it is over. In discussing the nature of decision making in curriculum development, Johnson proposes that it is "a continuing and cyclical process of development, revision, maintenance and renewal which needs to continue throughout the life of the curriculum." Similarly, teachers are involved in a cycle of decision making about their courses, as shown in Figure 1.

All teachers have experience with stage 2, teaching a course. Even when following an assigned text or syllabus, a teacher must still make decisions about what to emphasize, leave out, augment, and review and how to practice, how much, with whom, and when. Most teachers have experience with stages 3 and 4 because they teach the same course or use the same textbook one semester after another and change the way they teach according to their experience. For example, a teacher may decide to spend more time on pronunciation or on Unit 3 the next term because experience has shown that those are problem areas for her students. In this respect, planning and teaching lessons are a microversion of planning and teaching courses. The teacher who decides that in the 9:30 class the students needed more time to practice Exercise 3 and so gives the 11:30 class extra time is operating in a way similar to the teacher who determines that in the next term students will need to spend more time on Unit 3. A teacher's expertise at the level of planning and teaching lessons is thus both part of and similar to the overall process of course development.

Problematizing

When a teacher who is about to design a new course asks, "Are there any guidelines? Is there a procedure to follow?" the hoped-for answer is yes. No teacher wants to reinvent the wheel, and if there is a procedure to follow, she wants to know what it is. In practice, however, the answer to the questions is both yes and no: yes because there are models, guidelines, and principles to consider that can help a teacher make sense of her situation, mobilize her resources, and organize her progress; no because the guidelines are not a recipe. There is no set procedure to follow that will guarantee a successful course because each teacher and each teacher's situation is different. Put another way, there is no answer to give, but there is an answer to find.

A set of guidelines and principles will be the subject of the next chapter. They address the areas of needs assessment, goal and objective setting, conceptualizing and organizing content, choosing or adapting materials and activities, evaluation, and consideration of constraints and resources. Though they suggest an ordered process, it is probably more realistic to view them as a framework of components that overlap both conceptually and temporally and raise issues for the teacher to consider. Different teachers will start with different issues. One teacher may start by thinking about who the students are, another by figuring out what to do with the required material, and another by trying to formulate course goals and objectives.

Where a teacher starts in the process of course design depends on the constraints and resources of her situation and how she perceives them. To proceed, she needs to understand the givens of her situation, to identify the challenges that will shape her decisions, and to figure out what must and can be done. I call this process "problematizing" her situation.[2] Problematizing and problem solving are not the same. Problematizing depends on the teacher's perceptions of the context, out of which arise problems to be solved. The teacher defines the problems. Problem solving assumes that the problems are givens that the teacher needs to address. Asking questions and identifying problems are obvious means of problematizing. However, the process is not necessarily one that results in an articulated statement because most teachers work autonomously. When teachers problematize, they do so in concrete terms because the challenges arise from a concrete situation. The generic questions may be "What do I see as the challenges of

---

2 Problematizing derives from Paulo Freire's term *problematization,* about which he writes, "The process of problematization is basically someone's reflection on a content which results from an act, or reflection on the act itself in order to act better together with others within the framework of reality" (Freire 1973: 154).

my situation?" and "What resources are needed and are available to address the challenges?" but to teachers the questions sound more like "What kind of material works with teenagers?" or "How do I go about motivating the more advanced students in the class?" As a teacher problematizes her situation, she can begin to find workable solutions that make use of her experience and the resources available to her.

Problematizing requires that the teacher recognize the value of her own experience. Because of the role played by experience, there is no such thing as "starting a course from scratch." The expertise acquired through experience is an important source of answers as a teacher problematizes her situation. It is often difficult for teachers to acknowledge their own expertise; instead, they seek answers from people they consider experts. Valuable though the knowledge of experts may be, teachers themselves are experts in their settings, and their past experience and successes can serve as bridges to new situations. Correspondingly, the experience of developing a course enables teachers to make sense of the theories and expertise of others because it gives them opportunities to clarify their understanding of theory and make it concrete. Their practice in turn changes their understanding of the theories. For example, examining needs assessment tools, understanding the rationale of two different models for integrating content, or examining other course syllabuses can trigger the appropriate steps and solutions. In applying that new knowledge, the needs assessment is modified or expanded to fit the teacher's situation, a third way of putting together content emerges, or the course syllabuses are found to be inappropriate, which helps the teacher decide what is appropriate.

Finding one's own way in designing a course does not mean that all ways are equally effective. Successful course design depends on the teacher's making sense of what she is doing, not just doing it. Gaining access to one's expertise and that of others depends on a teacher's ability to make sense of her experience through reflection and understanding, to make a bridge between practice and thought so that one can influence the other. Teachers develop various tools to aid in reflection and analysis, including journals, notes, reading, conversation, and rest.

Just as they develop an approach to teaching that guides them in each new teaching situation, teachers develop an approach to course development that guides them in developing other courses. The approach is the result of experience, not a condition for it. The experience of developing a course is not always a clearly articulated, rational process. The approach one develops can eventually be articulated in rational terms, such as a series of steps or a framework. The rational look of a framework or plan is a later result of the process. The framework does not exist a priori. It evolves. Course development is a dynamic, ongoing process. The variables that make a context unique continue to change, as does the teacher. There is a continuous interaction of practice and the reflection that shapes it and is shaped by it. Thus an approach that can continue to serve in developing one's courses must be flexible.

The stories of six teachers as course developers

The teachers whose accounts make up the body of this book problematized their situations and developed courses in ways that made sense to them. Their stories are meant to serve as examples rather than as models. They are not case studies that have been constructed for specific purposes, such as those proposed by Shulman (1986): prototypes, which exemplify theoretical principles; precedents, which capture and communicate principles of practice or maxims; and parables, which convey norms or values. Rather they are accounts or stories of experience, told by the teachers who experienced them. I have chosen to use these stories as the focus of this book for several reasons. First, accounts such as these are useful in teacher education because they are a way of "capturing the complexity, specificity, and interconnectedness" of teachers' experiences (Carter 1993: 6). These accounts show teachers dealing with the unpredictable and contexual nature of course development issues as they occur in real situations. They illustrate the dilemmas faced by these teachers and the web of factors influencing their decisions. Second, they highlight various aspects of the framework in Chapter 2, and yet, because they are stories, they cannot be interpreted in one way and thus "cannot be subsumed into what Bruner (1985) called paradigmatic knowledge," which "requires consistency and noncontradiction" (Carter 1993: 7). Thus these stories contribute to our understanding of the framework components by presenting them to us embedded in the complexity of real situations. Finally, these concrete experiences provide readers with an opportunity to examine their own personal theories and test their own sense of plausibility.

The six teachers were asked to write a narrative in response to the following questions, which are based on the view of course development as a multistage process as illustrated in Figure 1.

1. What process did you follow in designing your course?
2. How did you modify the course once you started teaching it, and what prompted you to modify it?
3. In reviewing the process you went through in designing the course, what would you do differently, and why? (In other words, what have you learned about course design?)

The teachers are all experienced ESL or EFL teachers, with experience at the time of writing the narratives ranging from five to twenty years. The

Table 1 *Teachers and course features featured in this book*

Author	Chapter	Students	Type of course	Place
Johan Uvin	3	Health-care workers, Chinese	Workplace ESOL	Nursing home (U.S.)
Pat Fisher	4	Junior high (middle-school), multinational	Content-based social studies	International school (Japan)
Maria del Carmen Blyth	5	Postgraduate, Ecuadorian	English for academic purposes	Language institute (Ecuador)
Maria Estela Pinheiro Franco	6	High school, Brazilian	Writing supplement	Language institute (Brazil)
Barbara Fujiwara	7	University, Japanese	Advanced listening	Junior college (Japan)
Laura Hull	8	Business personnel, multinational	Individually tailored language training	Language institute (U.S.)

teachers and their situations were chosen to reflect a range of contexts in the field of English language teaching. Table 1 summarizes some of the characteristics of the courses they developed.

Six stories cannot possibly encompass all the contexts in the broad field of English language teaching, but they can illustrate a diversity of approaches to achieve a similar end, the development of a course. Moreover, these stories are meant to be examples from which the reader can learn and draw her own conclusions, not models that the reader is expected to emulate. The teachers approached their situations in different ways, not only because of the differences in the types of courses they were developing but also because of the differences in their contexts and their perceptions of the challenges of those contexts. In that sense, these six teachers are both representative and unique.

Suggestions for using this book

As this book is based on the two premises that course development is a grounded process and that teachers construct their understandings through the interaction of theory in the general sense, theory in the personal sense, and practice, one way to approach this book is with a course in mind, as a way of grounding what you read. The course can be one that you are developing or will develop or one that you have already taught. In reading about the framework of components in Chapter 2, you can use your chosen course to determine which aspects of the framework are useful and appropriate to work with, as well as which issues to explore. In reading the teachers' accounts and subsequent analyses, your own context will allow you to determine what is useful, notice things that you may not have thought of before, and consider other ways to approach course design. The tasks that follow each account are designed to be carried out with reference to your chosen context. The analysis follows rather than precedes each account so that you can interpret it in light of your own experience.

Another way to read this book is to choose one of the components in the framework and analyze the way in which each teacher addresses that component. For example, does each teacher assess students' needs? How? How does each teacher conceptualize content? How does each teacher deal with evaluation?

A third way is to use the following questions, which are based on the concept of problematizing:

1. What steps did this teacher follow in designing this course?
2. Where did this teacher start in the process? Why?
3. What did this teacher see as the main challenges or considerations in her situation?

4. What seem to be the beliefs, values and priorities of this teacher?
5. How did this teacher draw on her own experience and expertise?
6. How did this teacher gain a perspective on what she was doing so that she could make sense of it? What were her "breakthroughs," and how did they come about?
7. How did this teacher make sense of and use of the theories and expertise of others?
8. What are the characteristics of this teacher's approach to course design?
9. How will this teacher's approach serve her in the development of other courses?

Finally, you may simply wish to read the accounts as stories whose central figures are teachers engaged in understanding and shaping their teaching as they experience the setbacks, breakthroughs, problems, and accomplishments of developing a course.

References

Breen, M. 1987. Contemporary paradigms in syllabus design. *Language Teaching 20* (2–3): 81–92, 157–174.

Bruner, J. 1985. Narrative and paradigmatic modes of thought. In E. Eisner, ed., *Learning and Teaching the Ways of Knowing* (84th yearbook of the National Society for the Study of Education), pp. 97–115. Chicago: University of Chicago Press.

Carter, K. 1993. The place of story in the study of teaching and teacher education. *Educational Researcher 22* (1): 5–12, 18.

Colton, A. and G. Sparks-Langer. 1993. A conceptual framework to guide the development of teacher reflection and decision making. *Journal of Teacher Education 44* (1): 45–54.

Freire, P. 1973. *Education for Critical Consciousness.* New York: Seabury Press.

Hutchinson, T., and A. Waters. 1987. *English for Specific Purposes: A Learning-Centered Approach.* Cambridge: Cambridge University Press.

Johnson, R. K. 1989. A decision-making framework for the coherent language curriculum. In R. K. Johnson, ed., *The Second Language Curriculum,* pp. 1–23. Cambridge: Cambridge University Press.

Kennedy, M. 1991. *An Agenda for Research on Teacher Learning.* East Lansing: Michigan State University, National Center for Research on Teacher Learning.

Nunan, D. 1987. *The Teacher as Curriculum Developer.* Sydney: National Curriculum Resource Centre, Adult Migrant Education Program.

Prabhu, N. S. 1990. There is no best method. Why? *TESOL Quarterly 24:* 2.

Richards, J. 1990. *The Language Teaching Matrix.* New York: Cambridge University Press.

Shulman, L. 1986. Those who understand: Knowledge growth in teaching. *Educational Researcher 15* (2): 4–14.

White, R. V. 1988. *The ELT Curriculum: Design Innovation and Management.* Oxford: Blackwell.

Yalden, J. 1987. *Principles of Course Design for Language Teaching.* New York: Cambridge University Press.

2 A framework of course development processes

Kathleen Graves

Curriculum design specialists have developed various frameworks that break down the process of curriculum and course development into components and subprocesses (see, for example, Dubin and Olshtain 1986; Hutchinson and Waters 1987; Johnson 1989; Nunan 1985, 1988a, 1988b; Richards 1990; White 1988). A framework of components is useful for several reasons: It provides an organized way of conceiving of a complex process; it sets forth domains of inquiry for the teacher, in that each component puts forth ideas as well as raises issues for the teacher to pursue; it provides a set of terms currently used in talking about course development and thus a common professional vocabulary and access to the ideas of others. The framework described here, while drawing on the work of others, is cast in terms of my own work with teachers. It is not a framework of equal parts: Each individual's context determines which processes need the most time and attention. Furthermore, the processes are not necessarily sequential but may be carried on in the planning, teaching, and replanning stages of course development.

In Table 1, each component is identified and rephrased in question form to clarify its meaning.

Needs assessment

What are my students needs? How can I assess them so that I can address them?

What is needs assessment,[1] and why does a teacher undertake it? At its most basic, needs assessment involves finding out what the learners know and can do and what they need to learn or do so that the course can bridge the gap (or some part of it). Thus needs assessment involves seeking and interpreting information about one's students' needs so that the course will

1 The terms *needs analysis* and *needs assessment* are often used interchangeably. But as Susan Pomeroy once suggested to me, they refer to separate processes: Assessment involves obtaining data, whereas analysis involves assigning value to those data.

12

Table 1   *Framework components*

Needs assessment: *What are my students' needs? How can I assess them so that I can address them?*

Determining goals and objectives: *What are the purposes and intended outcomes of the course? What will my students need to do or learn to achieve these goals?*

Conceptualizing content: *What will be the backbone of what I teach? What will I include in my syllabus?*

Selecting and developing materials and activities: *How and with what will I teach the course? What is my role? What are my students' roles?*

Organization of content and activities: *How will I organize the content and activities? What systems will I develop?*

Evaluation: *How will I assess what students have learned? How will I assess the effectiveness of the course?*

Consideration of resources and constraints: *What are the givens of my situation?*

address them effectively. However, how one defines a student's needs is a complex issue open to interpretation. One way of conceptualizing needs is to distinguish between "objective" and "subjective" needs (Richterich 1980. Brindley (1989: 70) defines *objective needs* as "derivable from different kinds of factual information about learners, their use of language in real-life communication situations as well as their current language proficiency and language difficulties" and *subjective needs* as "the cognitive and affective needs of the learner in the learning situation, derivable from information about affective and coginitive factors such as personality, confidence, attitudes, learners' wants and expectations with regard to the learning of English and their individual cognitive style and learning strategies."

In assessing objective needs, one can include information about students' backgrounds – country and culture, education, family, profession, age, languages spoken, and so on; students' abilities or proficiency in speaking, understanding, reading, and writing English; and students' needs with respect to how they will use or deal with English outside of the classroom. In assessing subjective needs, one can include information about students' attitudes toward the target language and culture, toward learning, and toward themselves as learners; students' expectations of themselves and of the course; students' underlying purposes – or lack thereof – in studying English; and students' preferences with respect to how they will learn.

Different students have different needs, and the information gathered through needs assessment can help a teacher make choices as to what to teach and how to teach it. For example, students who wish to attend universities in English-speaking countries will have needs related to academic tasks and academic discourse. Objective information about their prior experience in academic settings, their level of English, and their field of study can contribute to the teacher's decisions about her course. Their subjective needs may be related to concerns about adjusting to the university setting and to a new culture, their level of self-confidence, or their expectations regarding what and how they will be taught. Subjective needs are often as important as objective needs. Teachers may find, as Johan Uvin (Chapter 3) did in his course for Chinese health-care workers, that unless subjective needs are taken into account, objective needs may not be met.

Who provides information about needs? Who determines the needs? A needs assessment can include input from students as well as from the various people connected to the course, such as teachers, funders, parents, administration, and employers. In a university ESL setting, for example, information from the students' future professors regarding what the students will be expected to read, research, and present can help the teacher shape her course (Tarone and Yule 1989). Teachers may have to work with a conception of needs determined by their institution or other party and conduct their assessment accordingly. The students' needs in Uvin's workplace ESOL course were initially defined by the institution as the language and behavior needed for the workers to function in their work setting.

When does one conduct a needs assessment? Depending on one's context, needs assessment can be conducted in stage 1, the planning stage; in stage 2, the teaching stage; and also in stage 3, the replanning stage, if one determines that the assessment must be modified in some way. Teachers who have contact with their students prior to teaching the course can undertake a precourse needs assessment. In many cases, however, a formal precourse needs assessment is neither necessary nor appropriate. Some teachers are able to make fairly accurate assumptions about their students' needs with respect to the course on the basis of prior experience with the course or with those particular students. In many cases, precourse assessment is simply not feasible because the teacher does not have contact with the students until the first day of class.

Another important factor in deciding when to assess needs is the teacher's view of the purpose of needs assessment. Needs assessment can also be a teaching tool because it can help students become more aware and more purposeful in their learning. Many teachers see it as an ongoing part of teaching, on the one hand, because it may take time to establish the kind of rapport with students that allows for a clear understanding of needs and, on the other, because they view it as a teaching tool that enables them to work in partnership with their students to determine needs and ensure that the course meets those needs.

Teachers who use needs assessment as an ongoing part of their classes develop activities that help students clarify and focus their needs. Such activities can include mindmapping (creating word maps) and student-generated questionnaires (Grant and Shank 1993). For example, in a writing class, students begin to articulate their needs based on a "mindmap" around the word *writing*. Teachers may use dialogue journals, discussion, or written responses to focus questions – for example, as suggested to me by Don Cherry, one's best and worst learning experiences. Many familiar activities can be given a needs assessment focus by the teacher.

How does one conduct a needs assessment? Teachers use a variety of methods. Questionnaires are a common needs assessment tool. They can be written in English or, when appropriate and feasible, in the native language of the students. One of the challenges in designing a questionnaire is choosing questions that will be interpreted correctly and will provide the information sought, especially if one is seeking subjective data. Interviews with students and others (such as employers or professors) are another common way of finding out students' needs. Other means include observation of or, in some cases, participation in the situations in which students will use English. Teachers may obtain samples of written materials, such as manuals or textbooks, that students will have to use. Stern (1992) cautions against gathering so much data that one cannot analyze and put it to use.

Tests and interviews that measure proficiency are also a part of needs assessment because they help determine what students already know and where they are lacking. Many institutions administer proficiency tests for placement purposes. Teachers may also design in-class activities for the first days of class that measure students' proficiency in reading, writing, speaking, or listening.

Hutchinson and Waters (1987: 54) make a distinction between *target needs* ("what the learner needs to do in the target situation") and *learning needs* ("what the learner needs to do in order to learn"). Needs assessment is clearly a sensible undertaking when students have target needs – real-life language needs and a context for using the language skills gained in class, as for immigrants to an English-speaking country, students studying or planning to study in English-speaking schools, or people who use English in their work. However, even when needs are clear, as with immigrants learning to function in a new culture, they may be so general that the teacher has to find ways to assess and define them so that they can be translated into realistic goals. The challenge becomes focusing the needs assessment so as to provide adequate but not overwhelming data on which to base decisions.

In other contexts – particularly, but not only, EFL contexts – teachers face a different problem because many of their students have no target needs, no clearly anticipated use for the skills gained through study. English may be a requirement for an exit or entrance exam. It may be viewed as a subject like math or science, or it may be a social undertaking like the study of music. For these students, the notion of needs outside the classroom is tenuous. The focus of the needs assessment shifts to the learning needs or subjective needs of the students so as to increase motivation and to help students find purpose and interest in what they are doing in the course. For example, Gorsuch (1991) describes a technique for helping students in a conversation class in Japan articulate their needs and set periodic and achievable goals to meet those needs.

Issues

Needs assessment is not a value-free process. It is influenced by the teacher's view of what the course is about, the institutional constraints, and the students' perceptions of what is being asked of them. For example, one teacher of immigrants might ask them to list situations in which they use or expect to use English, with the aim of providing instruction in the language and behavior necessary to deal with those situations. Another teacher might ask the same students to articulate or enact problems they face in adjusting to the new culture, with the aim of helping them exert control over the acculturation process.

For many students, needs assessment is an unfamiliar procedure, and they may have difficulty articulating their purposes or needs. The process itself may engender uncertainty in the students, as knowing their needs is presumably the responsibility of the teacher or institution. Questions may be interpreted differently by different students or may not elicit the anticipated answers. Students' perceptions of needs may not match those of the teacher. The teacher's view of the students' needs may conflict with those of the institution.

The content and method of needs assessment should be evaluated as to appropriateness and effectiveness in achieving their purpose of identifying the needs of the students. It may take several tries to develop effective needs assessment tools. Those tools should not be viewed as "one time only" processes. Needs assessment should be viewed as an ongoing process, both in its development and in its use.

Determining goals and objectives

What are the purposes and intended outcomes of the course? What will my students need to do or learn to achieve these goals?

What are goals and objectives and what is the relationship between them? Goals are general statements of the overall, long-term purposes of the course. Objectives express the specific ways in which the goals will be achieved. The goals of a course represent the destination; the objectives, the various points that chart the course toward the destination. To arrive at the destination, one must pass each of these points. Let us consider the example of Chapter 4, Pat Fisher's social studies course for seventh-grade ESOL students. Objectives permit Fisher to define her goals more precisely by breaking them down into concrete and achievable teaching and learning activities. For example, one of Fisher's goals is to orient her students to the particular skills, vocabulary, and rhetorical styles of the social sciences. Some of the objectives that help move the children toward that goal are for students to "be able to read maps, graphs, and charts with demonstrated understanding" and "to know the geographic, topical, and climatic features of the major regions of the Eastern Hemisphere."

Why set goals and objectives? Setting goals and objectives provides a sense of direction and a coherent framework for the teacher in planning her course. Breaking goals down into objectives is very much like making a map of the territory to be explored. It is a way for the teacher to conceptualize her course in terms of teachable chunks. Clear goals and objectives give the teacher a basis for determining which content and activities are appropriate for her course. They also provide a framework for evaluation of the effectiveness or worth of an activity: Did it help students achieve or make progress toward the goals and objectives? Clearly, there are many routes (objectives) to a given destination, some more circuitous than others, and the length and nature of the route will depend on one's departure point.

How does one choose appropriate goals and objectives? There is no simple answer to this question. To arrive at the goals, one asks the question, "What are the purposes and intended outcomes of the course?" The answer may be influenced by an analysis of students' needs, the policies of the institution, and the way the teacher conceptualizes content, among other factors. Stern (1992) proposes four types of goals for language learners: proficiency goals, cognitive goals, affective goals, and transfer goals. Proficiency goals include general competency, mastery of the four skills (speaking, listening, reading, and writing), or mastery of specific language behaviors. Cognitive goals include mastery of linguistic knowledge and mastery of cultural knowledge. Affective goals include achieving positive attitudes and feelings about the target language, achieving confidence as a user of the language, and achieving confidence in oneself as a learner. Transfer goals involve learning how to learn so that one can call upon learning skills gained in one situation to meet future learning challenges. Thus goals may address not only the attainment of knowledge and skills but also the development of attitude and awareness.

Goals should also be realizable. Richards (1990: 3) gives the example of a goal stated as "Students will develop favorable attitudes toward the program." He goes on to point out, "However, while this goal might represent a sincere wish on the part of teachers, it should appear as a program goal only if it is to be addressed concretely in the program."

The formulation of objectives provides the check as to whether the goals will be addressed. To arrive at objectives, one asks, "What do students need to learn or do to achieve these purposes?" One of the challenges in formulating objectives is thinking of objectives that are congruent with the goals and that are not so narrow that they enmesh the teacher in an unnecessary level of detail.

How does one state objectives? As Nunan (1988b: 60) has pointed out, "Objectives are really nothing more than a particular way of formulating or stating content and activities." Thus how one conceptualizes and states objectives depends on how one conceptualizes the content of the course. Content as knowledge might be stated as "Students will know . . . ," "Students will learn the . . . ," or "Students will learn that . . ." Content as skill might be stated as "Students will be able to . . . ," "Students will know how to . . . ," or "Students will develop the ability to . . . ," Performance or behavioral objectives are most often associated with content as skill; however, this represents a narrow view as they specify terminal behavior rather than the development of skills, such as those needed to read, write, listen and speak effectively (Richards 1990). Content as attitude and awareness would be stated as "Students will be aware that . . . ," "Students will develop an awareness of . . . ," "Students will develop an attitude of . . . ," or "Students will explore their attitudes towards . . ." Objectives stated in this way can help teachers address affective aspects of learning.

The examples given suggest what students will know, know how to do, or be aware of as a result of the course. Objectives may also be stated in terms of what students will do in the course. Saphier and Gower (1987) list five kinds of objectives, all interrelated. The first three concern what students will do; the last two, what they will have mastered.

1. *Coverage objectives* articulate what will be covered. Example: *We will cover the first five units of the course book.*
2. *Activity objectives* articulate what the students will do. Examples: *Students will write six different kinds of paragraphs. Students will do paragraph development exercises.*
3. *Involvement objectives* articulate how to maximize student involvement and interest. Examples: *Students will engage in discussions about which paragraphs they like best. Students will brainstorm lists of interesting topics to write about.*

4. *Mastery objectives* articulate what students will be able to do as a result of their time in class. Example: *Students will be able to write an interesting paragraph that contains a topic sentence and supporting details.*
5. *Critical thinking objectives* articulate which learning skills students will develop. Example: *Students will be able to determine characteristics of a good paragraph and say why they think a paragraph is good.*

Tension often exists between coverage objectives and mastery objectives because the time it takes to master skills or knowledge or to develop awareness may not correspond to the time allotted in a syllabus. This tension can create dilemmas for teachers who must cover and test the material in the syllabus yet wish to ensure that students have mastered the material prior to moving on. The tension can also put teachers at odds with their students or the insitution if the teacher believes that success is achieved through demonstrated mastery but the students expect coverage to *mean* mastery.

Issues

The main issue is that many teachers do not formulate goals and objectives at all or do so only after having thought about what they will teach and how. Studies on teacher planning underscore this fact (Clark and Peterson 1986). My own work with teachers has shown that they consider the setting of goals and objectives a valuable process but one that they find difficult to articulate and organize. They feel that they must first be clear about what they are teaching and how they view the content. They report from experience that they cannot clearly formulate their goals and objectives until after they have taught the course at least once. (Returning to the map analogy, one cannot map a route until one has traveled it.) Thus for many teachers, this is not the entry point into the process of course development.

Another issue involves clarity with respect to students' needs. It is easier to set goals in situations where these needs are clear; otherwise, the goals of the course may shift and be redefined as the course progresses. Finally, goals and objectives are a statement of intent, subject to reexamination and change once the course is under way.

Conceptualizing content

What will be the backbone of what I teach? What will I include in my syllabus?
When a teacher conceptualizes content, she is figuring out which aspects

of language and language learning she will include, emphasize, and integrate in her course. This is not the relatively simple process it once was. Two decades ago, language teaching was still heavily influenced by a structural view of language (Richards and Rodgers 1986). This influence resulted in a "one size fits all" approach to content and methods, meaning that, for example, an EFL teacher could use the same textbook and the same drills or pattern practice for factory workers, college students, and housewives. There was not much question about content: It was grammatical structures and vocabulary.

Much has changed in recent years in the fields of applied linguistics and language acquisition and in approaches to language teaching. The proficiency movement, the concept and various models of communicative competence, the advent of ESP (English for specific purposes), the proliferation of methods of language teaching, and the diversification of the population of English learners have all provided the teacher with many more options to consider in deciding what will be the backbone of her course (Canale 1983; Hutchinson and Waters 1987; Omaggio Hadley 1993; Richards 1990; Savignon 1983; Yalden 1987). Now the choices a teacher makes are much more context-dependent and so involve a number of factors such as who the students are, their goals and expectations in learning English, the teacher's own conception of what language is and what will best meet the students' needs, the nature of the course, and the institutional curriculum. A course for immigrants in an English-speaking country will likely stress different content than a course for high school students in their own country. A course for college students on vacation in an English-speaking country will likely stress different content than a course for the same students preparing to enter a university there.

Let us look at some ways of conceptualizing and categorizing content. The boundaries between categories are permeable; they overlap conceptually and are not exclusive of each other. The teacher's challenge is to figure out which ones are appropriate for her course and how she will integrate them. They will be described and then outlined in a syllabus grid, which will be added to with each successive component. In my experience, teachers do not usually use syllabus grids to lay out the content of a course (only one teacher in this volume has done so), but a grid is a graphic way to illustrate possible categories.

The traditional way of conceptualizing content, which many teachers have experienced in their own learning of language, is as grammar structures, sentence patterns, and vocabulary. These aspects of language are relatively systematic and rule-governed and are often the basis of content found in textbooks. They include rules of word formation (morphology), rules of pronunciation (phonology), and grammatical structures and relationships among words at the sentence level (syntax). A syllabus grid that includes these aspects of language might look like this:

Grammar	Pronunciation	Vocabulary

For language teachers, the possibilities for what to include in a syllabus opened up with the advent of what has come to be called the communicative approach (Larsen-Freeman 1986). The work of sociolinguists such as Hymes (1972) and Halliday (1973, 1975) and of applied linguists such as Wilkins (1976) and Van Ek (1975) has helped reorient thinking about the nature of language. The communicative approach is based on ideas about language, on the one hand, and about the purposes of language learning, on the other. Language is used in a context, which determines and constrains the choices that language users make with respect to purpose, style, register, and topic. Learners must use the language and have purposes for using it. From the point of view of conceptualizing content, the communicative approach added several dimensions. First, it added the dimension of language functions, such as to apologize, to persuade, to convey information. It also added the dimension of notions, which form a continuum from general concepts such as time, space, and relationship to specific topic-related notions such as house and home, weather, and personal identification (Van Ek 1975). Language was seen as being used for communicative purposes in situations with other people, which call on the learner to pay attention to both the content of the language and its appropriateness with respect to formality, non-verbal behavior, tone, and so on. Communicative situations might include ordering food in a restaurant, buying stamps at the post office, extending an invitation to a social event. Thus we can add these categories to our syllabus grid:

Functions	Notions and topics	Communicative situations
Grammar	Pronunciation	Vocabulary

The proficiency movement and the development of proficiency guidelines have emphasized a four-skills-based approach to syllabus design (Omaggio Hadley 1993). For some teachers, these skills are a given, as students have to use some combination of speaking, listening, reading, and writing in class. However, because becoming proficient in each of these skills entails mastery of a set of subskills and processes, many teachers choose to emphasize certain skills or find ways to integrate them. For example, to become proficient in writing, a student must learn how to structure paragraphs, how to use cohesive devices, the rhetorical styles of written English, editing techniques and so on. Two of the teachers in this book describe courses devoted primarily to developing one skill, writing in Chapter 6 and listening in Chapter 7. Thus we can add the following categories to our syllabus grid:

Listening skills	Speaking skills	Reading skills	Writing skills
Functions		Notions and topics	Communicative situations
Grammar		Pronunciation	Vocabulary

The emphasis on communicative competence as based on and brought about by interaction has prompted a view of language as not just something one learns but something one *does*. Thus teachers may conceive of their syllabus in terms of what the students will do in the classroom as activities or tasks. Tasks have been variously defined. Prabhu (1987: 24) defines a task as an activity that requires learners "to arrive at an outcome from given information through some process of thought," such as deciding on an itinerary based on train timetables or composing a telegram to send to someone. Tasks have also been defined as projects in which learners work together to produce something, such as a putting together a newspaper or conducting a survey (Hutchinson 1984). Nunan (1989) proposes a task continuum, with real-world tasks at one end and pedagogic tasks at the other. Real-world tasks ask students to use language in ways that they might outside the classroom, such as listening to the radio, reading the newspaper, or using a train schedule. Pedagogic tasks are ones that would not occur outside of the classroom but help students develop skills necessary to function in that world, such as information gap activities.

The competency-based approach to syllabus design was developed in the United States in response to the influx of immigrants in the 1970s and 1980s. It is a combination of the communicative and task-based approaches and has been used in courses for teaching immigrants, who have immediate needs with respect to functioning in English in the community and in the workplace. Competencies are "task-oriented goals written in terms of be-havioral objectives that include language behavior" (Center for Applied Linguistics, 1983: 9). They are the language and behavior necessary to function in situations related to living in the community and finding and maintaining a job. Competencies related to living in the community have also been called *life-skills*. Those related to jobs have been called *vocational skills*. (See, for example, the California ESL Model Standards for adult education 1993.)

However one defines them, tasks can be geared to one's specific group of learners. For business personnel, tasks might include giving a business presentation or writing a report; for university students, tasks might include writing a research paper or preparing a report from notes taken at a lecture. In Chapter 5, Carmen Blyth describes the development of an EAP (English for academic purposes) course for postgraduate students in which she conceptualizes content in terms of academic tasks, such as listening to lectures, and the skills necessary to carry out such tasks, such as note taking and listening for gist. We can add two other categories to our syllabus grid:

		Tasks and activities		Competencies
Listening skills	Speaking skills	Reading skills	Writing skills	
Functions	Notions and topics		Communicative situations	
Grammar	Pronunciation		Vocabulary	

The role of culture in language learning is receiving increasing attention. Culture provides a broader and deeper context for how one knows or determines what is valued, appropriate, or even feasible and why. Damen (1986) calls culture the "fifth dimension of language teaching." Kramsch (1993) asserts that culture is not just a fifth skill or even an aspect of communicative competence but the underlying dimension of all one knows and does. One teacher, Victoria Northridge, described culture to me as "the piece that makes everything else 'make sense', that enables connections to be made between the language and how to use it, when to use it, whom to expect it from, and what kind of response to expect after you use it." Thus a teacher who views culture as an integral part of a syllabus might include the development of awareness of the role culture plays in human interaction, how to understand and interpret the cultural aspects of language and behavior, and the development of skills in behaving and responding in culturally appropriate ways in addition to knowledge of the target culture.

The learning of language through or in conjunction with subject matter can also be the focus of a language course. Such courses have been called *content-based* because they integrate "particular content with language teaching aims" (Brinton, Snow, and Wesche 1989). Such content may be school- or work-related — for example, history, economics, or computer technology. A content-based course may teach the subject matter directly or use subject matter as the basis for language-learning lessons. Thus the target language can be both a means for and a by-product of learning the subject matter. Content-based approaches play a critical role in bilingual programs for children as well as in ESP courses and, increasingly, in EAP courses. We can add culture and content to our syllabus grid:

		Content	
Culture	Tasks and activities	Competencies	
Listening skills	Speaking skills	Reading skills	Writing skills
Functions	Notions and topics	Communicative situations	
Grammar	Pronunciation	Vocabulary	

Another major change in how teachers conceptualize content has come about because of the view that one teaches learners, not just language. The emphasis on the learner has introduced other important elements into a teacher's conception of what she will teach: the learner's affect, which includes attitudes, self-confidence, and motivation, and the learner's approach to learning, which includes both understanding and developing one's learning skills. How to improve learners' self-confidence or helping learners become aware of their attitude toward the target culture may be explicitly included in a syllabus, as may activities that help learners become aware of their strengths and overcome their weaknesses as learners. The development of definitions, taxonomies, and methods of developing learning strategies is one way in which the emphasis on helping learners become self-aware has influenced syllabus design (O'Malley and Chamot 1990; Oxford 1990). Fisher (Chapter 4) combines elements from a content-based approach, a learner-training-based approach, and an academic language-based approach in her syllabus for her social studies ESL course. For each area – language, content, and strategies – she lists objectives for developing students' awareness and attitudes, knowledge and skills.

For some teachers, enabling students to participate in determining the content of their course so that what they do in class gives them the tools to cope with and change what they will encounter outside of the classroom is the focus of their course. Thus they ask the learners to engage in participatory processes that help them understand the social context of their problems and take control of their personal and professional lives through work in the classroom (Auerbach 1993; Auerbach and Wallerstein 1987). The problem-posing and experiential learning techniques described by Uvin in Chapter 3 illustrate this approach to syllabus design.

We can now add two more categories to the syllabus grid, learning strategies and participatory processes. The completed grid is shown in Figure 1.

Issues

Teaching involves making choices. It is not possible to teach a syllabus that explicitly encompasses all the areas mentioned here so teachers must

Participatory processes *Examples:* problem posing, experiential learning techniques		Learning strategies *Examples:* self-monitoring, problem identification, note taking	Content *Examples:* academic subjects, technical subjects	
Culture *Examples:* culture awareness, culture behavior, culture knowledge		Tasks and activities *Examples:* information gap activities, projects, skills or topic-oriented tasks such as giving a speech or making a presentation	Competencies *Examples:* applying for a job, renting an apartment	
Listening skills *Examples:* listening for gist, listening for specific information, inferring topic, choosing appropritae response	Speaking skills *Examples:* turn-taking, compensating for misunderstandings, using cohesive devices	Reading skills *Examples:* scanning for information, skimming for gist, understanding rhetorical devices	Writing skills *Examples:* using appropriate rhetorical style, using cohesive devices, structuring paragraphs	
Functions *Examples:* apologizing, disagreeing, persuading		Notions and topics *Examples:* time, quantity, health, personal identification	Communicative situations *Examples:* ordering in a restaurant, buying stamps at the post office	
Grammar *Examples:* structures (tense, pronouns), patterns (questions)		Pronunciation *Examples:* segmentals (phonemes, syllables), suprasegmentals (stress, rhythm, intonation)	Vocabulary *Examples:* word formation (suffixes, prefixes), collocation, lexical sets	

Figure 1   The completed syllabus grid

decide which categories make sense to them for a given course. The categories also overlap, both conceptually and in the classroom. For example, pronunciation is an important part of speaking skills. Vocabulary development is a part of notions and topics. Learning strategies can be linked to specific skills. Some of the categories are vast and can be divided into several subcategories. Many readers will find that they would label or define the categories differently or that certain categories are missing. For example, some teachers conceptualize content thematically.

Teachers of courses whose content has already been specified will face different issues. They may find that the breadth of content is unrealistic for the amount of time they have to teach it or that the way content has been defined is inappropriate, in their view, for the purposes of the course. The overlapping nature of the categories may be an aid in finding ways to adapt the existing content to their vision of the course.

Selecting and developing materials and activities

How and with what will I teach the course? What is my role? What are my students' roles?

For many teachers, course development starts not with determining objectives or conceptualizing content but with ideas about the course in action. They think about material they will use, activities their students will do, techniques they will employ. They think about the way they want their students to learn and their own role in the classroom. As Barbara Fujiwara puts it in Chapter 7, "Though now I do try to articulate objectives, my method of planning still begins with activities and visions of the class."

For many teachers, the material they use forms the backbone of the course. It is something concrete that students use, and it provides a focus for the class. Choosing material may mean development of new material when teaching a course for which there are no suitable materials, collecting a variety of materials, or adapting existing materials. Teachers consider a variety of factors in developing, choosing, or adapting materials. Two of the most important are their effectiveness in achieving the purposes of the course and their appropriateness for the students – and the teacher. Appropriateness includes student comfort and familiarity with the material, language level, interest, and relevance. Some teachers incorporate instruction in how to use unfamiliar materials as part of their course design. Feasibility and availability are also important to consider. In Chapter 7, Fujiwara describes a situation in which a text that seemed right in achieving the purposes of the course, developing listening skills and strategies, was in practice too difficult for the students and hence not appropriate at all.

Developing new materials and activities for using them requires time and a clear sense of why they will be used, how, and by whom. Because of the lack of time, teachers are often constrained or prefer to adapt existing materials. Maria Estela Pinheiro (Chapter 6) had the time to develop the materials for a writing supplement to the existing teen courses in her school. Her sense of purpose derived from the skill being learned, writing; her understanding of the writing process; and her perception that students needed to feel prepared with each step, to feel that the material was relevant to them, and to interact with one another in using it. Consequently, she developed materials that met those criteria.

Experienced teachers often develop a set of core materials and activities that they adapt each time they teach a course. The materials themselves are flexible and can be used in a number of ways, depending on the target skills or competencies. For example, newspaper articles can be used as a basis for developing reading skills, expanding vocabulary, or discussing culture. Pictures can be used as a focus for learning grammar or as a starting point for a writing assignment. Core activities are related to the way the teacher conceptualizes the content. A teacher may have a repertoire of activities for teaching pronunciation or for having students learn to understand cultural differences. For some teachers, materials and activities are integrated into a method, such as the Language Experience Approach (Rigg 1989). The emphasis on proficiency and learning language in context has led many teachers to use as much authentic material as possible in their classes (Omaggio Hadley 1993). For content-based courses, authentic material is the foundation. In Chapter 5, Blyth prepares for her EAP course by making a list of both materials and activities that students can use to develop their academic skills. She will then choose from these materials as her course progresses.

For teachers who are required to use a certain text, course development *is* the adaptation of the text, for the content of the text determines the content of the course. However, the text is not the course; rather, what the teacher and students do with the text constitutes the course. Textbooks are tools that can be figuratively cut up into component pieces and then rearranged to suit the needs, abilities, and interests of the students in the course. The material in a textbook can be modified to incorporate activities that will motivate students and move them beyond the constraints of the text. Das (1988: viii) points out that materials should not "pre-specify learning outcomes or attempt to control or substantially guide learning: their function is primarily to provide opportunities for learning through interaction."

The question "How will I teach?" also encompasses a teacher's approach and how she views her role and that of the learners. How much initiative will the students be expected to take, and toward what end? How will the students be asked to interact? The emphasis on learner awareness and concern for extending learning beyond the classroom have made the role of the learner a central focus of how a course is taught. Teachers design courses with activities and materials that have the students take a more active role in reflecting on their learning, determining the content of the course, and pursuing projects of interest to them. Such an approach may facilitate the search for materials in that the emphasis is not on the materials themselves but on what the students do with them.

Issues

For some teachers, the lack of materials is a challenge; for others, it is an opportunity. Developing materials requires time before, during, and after the course – for preparing, using, and modifying them, respectively. Yet having to use certain materials may produce the dilemma of coping with a text that does not meet students' needs or does not promote the teacher's

view of the roles of learners and teachers. Other aspects of course development, such as needs assessment and objective setting, may help the teacher
see how to adapt unsuitable materials and to what extent. Eventually, all
materials are adapted or modified in some way. Even materials that have
been developed by teachers for specific courses will be modified over time.

Organization of content and activities

*How will I organize the content and activities? What systems will I
develop?*

Regardless of whether one follows a fixed sequence or adopts a more
fluid approach to the order in which one teaches the content, part of course
development is figuring out systems for organizing the course. Systems can
focus on the lesson level (the organization of each lesson) and on the course
level (the overall organization of the course). We will look first at specific
considerations in sequencing material and then at considerations of the
overall organization of the course.

Two general, complementary principles of sequencing are building and
recycling. In deciding how to sequence material, one considers building
from the simple to the complex, from more concrete to more open-ended or
so that unit or activity A prepares students for unit or activity B. Building
from the simple to the complex in a writing course may mean learning how
to write narrative prose before developing an argumentative paper. In an
introductory language course, it may mean learning the numbers 1 to 9 to
use telephone numbers and then learning the numbers 10 to 60 to tell time.
Building from more concrete to more open-ended in a writing course may
mean that students first unscramble and discuss a sample paragraph before
writing their own paragraph. In an introductory language course, it may
mean talking about a family in a textbook picture using prescribed vocabulary before talking about one's own family.

Conceiving of activities as building blocks puts them in a "feeding"
relation where one activity feeds into another "if it provides something that
is needed for the second one . . . or the second exercise could not be done
unless the first had already been completed" (Low 1989: 145). For example, in a reading unit, students predict the content from pictures or headings
that accompany the text before actually reading the text. Or prior to a
restaurant role-playing activity, students learn menu items and the language
for ordering food.

The principle of recycling material means that students encounter previous material in new ways: in a new skill area, in a different type of
activity, or with a new focus. For example, material encountered in a

listening activity may be recycled in a writing exercise. Material encountered in an individual reading activity may be recycled in a role play with other students. Material about the target culture may be recycled in an activity about one's own culture. This approach to recycling material assumes that each new encounter with the material provides a challenge to students, thereby maintaining their interest and motivation. Recycling has the effect of integrating material and thus augments students' ability to use or understand it.

Sequencing occurs on the macro level of the course, as well as on the micro level of a week or unit or lesson within a course. In Chapter 6, Pinheiro describes sequencing the activities and materials for her writing course within each level, going from more concrete to more open-ended activities, as well as from one level to the next, requiring progressively longer and more difficult essays.

Two complementary ways to approach the overall organization of a course are as a cycle or as a matrix. Both approaches suggest a core of material to be learned and activities to be conducted within a given time frame. In the cyclical approach, a regular cycle of activities follows a consistent sequence. For example, in Chapter 7, for her advanced listening course, Fujiwara divides each session into three parts, the first for discussion of the homework assignment, the second for student presentations, and the third for watching and discussing a video. Pinheiro (Chapter 6) follows a cycle of activities for writing that reflects the steps of the writing process. The experiential learning cycle, as interpreted by Kolb (1984), has also been used as the basis for a cyclical approach to course organization (Shafiqi 1991).

In a matrix approach, the teacher works with a set of possible activities for a given time frame and, as the course progresses, decides which activities to work with. In Chapter 5, for her EAP course, Blyth describes such a situation, in which she compiles a list of possible activities and materials and then decides which to use, depending on her students' interests as well as the availability of the materials.

The cycle and the matrix are not mutually exclusive; many teachers use elements of both. Certain features in a course may be predictable, augmented by other elements drawn from a matrix, depending on the situation. Teachers who work with a fixed syllabus, such as that in a textbook, may nevertheless follow a cycle in the way they work with the material. Adapting material often means approaching it as a matrix from which to select, depending on one's students. Many teachers also set up certain daily or weekly rituals. For example, some teachers begin each session with a warm-up or review. Some teachers begin each week with a student presentation or end each week with an oral feedback session. All of these methods of organization permit a teacher to give a shape to her course.

Issues

Although the order in which the content and materials are taught may be determined prior to teaching the course, it may also be determined and modified as the course progresses. For some teachers, a negotiated syllabus, in which teacher and students decide together what they will learn, is preferable. In such cases, a predetermined sequence is seen as a handicap as it does not allow teachers to take into account the particular group of students in their course. In such a course, the sequence is not determined beforehand. Rather, the teacher has a map of the possible territory and works with the students to determine where it is most useful for them to go and in what order. Where a syllabus is provided, achieving flexibility is an issue.

Evaluation

How will I assess what students have learned? How will I assess the effectiveness of the course?

For most teachers, evaluation means evaluation *within* the course: assessing students' proficiency, progress, or achievement. How proficient are students in listening? Are students improving their writing skills? Have they learned to function in English in the workplace? Teachers build in some form of student evaluation when developing a course, ranging from formal tests to informal assessments. Hughes (1989) discusses four purposes for testing: to measure proficiency, to diagnose specific strengths and weaknesses, to place students in a course or program, and to assess their achievement in a course or program. The same testing instrument may be used for more than one purpose. For example, the TOEFL test is used by graduate programs in the United States as a proficiency test, but it is sometimes used as an achievement test if students show a gain on a TOEFL posttest. An oral entrance interview for placement purposes may also be used as an exit interview for purposes of assessing achievement. However, tests are not the only means teachers have to assess their students. Teachers may structure their classroom activities so that they can assess their students while the students participate. They may use a portfolio approach, in which students put together a portfolio of their work (Fingeret 1993). They may involve their students in deciding what should be assessed and how (Hull 1992).

Evaluation in course development also includes evaluation of the course itself. Was the course effective? In what ways? Where did it fall short? Such an evaluation may not be directly linked to assessment of student progress, although student evaluation and test results can provide feedback on the effectiveness of the course. If the students do well on tests or are judged to have made progress, presumably the course has been effective. But if students do not make progress or do not demonstrate a certain level of achievement, the effectiveness of the course may be questioned. Finding where the fault lies would be one of the purposes of course evaluation and could involve having students suggest why they did not make the progress expected.

Why does one evaluate? Generally speaking, a course is evaluated to promote and improve its effectiveness. This may be an internal matter, as when the teacher is concerned with developing the best course possible, in which case the evaluation is done largely for the benefit of the students and the teacher. However, courses are also evaluated to provide documentation for policy reasons, such as continued funding or retention in the curriculum. In such cases, evaluation is an external matter, and the teacher may be required to use certain methods of evaluation or to document the effectiviness of the course in a manner prescribed by an outside party. In Chapter 3, Johan Uvin describes how the need to document the effectiveness of his workplace course for the funding source influenced the development of the course. Similarly, the importance of accountability to the corporate client influenced the way Laura Hull (Chapter 8) developed her curriculum framework.

What can be evaluated? Any part of the process of course development can be evaluated, including the assumptions about and analysis of students' needs or backgrounds, goals and objectives, materials and activities, means of assessing students' progress, student participation, student roles, and the teacher's role. Thus each element of the framework is itself subject to evaluation. Was the needs assessment effective? Did I seek the right input, and did it enable me to make appropriate decisions about the course? If not, why not? Were the goals and objectives appropriate and achievable? Should they be changed? Did students find the material appropriately challenging, or was it too easy or too difficult? Were the activities appropriate? Did all students participate easily? Did I find suitable ways to evaluate students' progress? Did the tests test what had been learned?

When does one evaluate? In curriculum design, a distinction is usually made between *formative evaluation,* which takes place during the development and implementation of the curriculum for purposes of modifying it as it is being developed, and *summative evaluation,* which takes place after the curriculum has been implemented, for purposes of evaluating its success and improving it for future implementation (Brown 1989). A teacher who is involved in each stage of course design can think of evaluation as an ongoing part of the entire process. Thus evaluation can occur in the planning and teaching stages of the course, after it is over, and when it is replanned and retaught. In Chapter 8, Hull sets up systems of inquiry into the corporate language program she is directing, which enable her to re-form the program into a coherent curriculum.

Who evaluates? At the course level, the teacher and the students are the principal evaluators. However, administrators, funders, parents, and clients may have a role in evaluation, and their role may influence the shape or existence of the course. In Chapter 8, Hull describes how she sought input from the corporations who sent their employees, the employees who took the courses, and the teachers to determine how to set up the most effective program. In Chapter 3, Uvin describes the way in which the funder's expectations influence the method of evaluation as well as the existence of the course.

How does one evaluate? A variety of ways are available. A teacher's most important means is close observation of what students do in class and how they do it. If students have great difficulty performing certain tasks, one might be wise to question the appropriateness of the objectives or the activities. Informal chats with students can often provide as much informa-tion as responses to formal questionnaires. Teachers can also provide time for students to give written or oral input regarding specific aspects of the course. For example, some teachers hold regular oral feedback sessions with their students; and others have students write in journals. The teacher's own reflection and self-questioning play an important role in evalution.

Issues

Teachers tend to avoid extensive evaluation because they feel inadequate to a task in what they consider is the domain of "experts," for which special training in systematic analysis is necessary. Teachers must become familiar with the various purposes and types of testing, but they must also devise their own systems and areas of inquiry. As with needs assessment, teachers must experiment with different methods of evalution and monitor the suc-cess of each so as to maximize the effectiveness of their courses.

Consideration of resources and constraints

What are the givens of my situation?

Resources and constraints are two ways of looking at the same thing. A required course book may be a constraint for one teacher and a resource for another. A class of fewer than ten students may be a resource for one teacher and a constraint for another. Though these givens may seem sec-ondary to the processes just described, in fact they play a primary role in the development of a course because it is in considering the givens that a teacher begins to make sense of processes such as needs assessment and material selection. I have referred to this earlier as problematizing: defining the challenges of one's situation so that one can make decisions about what to do. In the absence of problematizing, a teacher may seek to graft solutions appropriate to another unique situation onto her situation. This became clear to me in the case of an EFL teacher who faced an extraordinary challenge: designing a conversation class for 140 students in a space meant for half as many. She felt that having examples of needs analysis questionnaires would be a key to developing her course. To me, this was an example of a teacher seeking answers from outside without having first specifically defined the challenges of her own situation. Such problematizing could eventually result in an examination of how others approached needs analysis as an aid in developing her own. Here is a sketch of one way of problematizing this teacher's situation:

- *This is a conversation class, but there are 140 students in a space that fits 70.* I need to look at ways of working within the constraints of the classroom such as ways to group or rotate students.
- *What kinds of conversations can 140 students possibly have?* I need to assess their language ability (*At what level can they carry on a conversation?*) and find out about their background and interests (*What can they have conversations about?*). How will I go about doing that? What kinds of questions should I ask them? If the assessment shows that their ability is low, I need to focus on the kind of preparation and foundation work necessary for conversations to take place.
- *How can I get them to work together to have these conversations?* Classroom management is an issue. I need to look at available materials with carefully structured activities as a means of classroom management. Or perhaps I could ask other teachers what has worked for them in this situation.
- *How can I monitor their activity?* I need to examine my role in the classroom. I also need to think about the types of monitoring and evaluation mechanisms I will use in the class.
- *What has worked in the past?* I need to think about the activities or classes in which I felt that things went well. Why did they go well? What can I take from those successes and build into this course?

These are questions that I propose. Were the teacher to go through a similar process, she might ask different ones or respond to the same ones in different ways because of her intimate knowledge of her context and her role in it. For example, how students are graded, whether there is a required text, and attendance patterns would all influence the kinds of questions she would ask. I included the question about past successes because teachers carry their experience over from one context to the next, and being able to understand what has been successful and why can provide a foundation for planning a course. In the context under discussion, the teacher had already taught the course and thus could be realistic in her expectations about what she could hope to accomplish with this group of students.

The constraints and resources of one's situation take many forms, some tangible, others not. Teachers work with or without physical and material resources such as books, technology, a classroom, and furniture. The lack of physical resources may encourage a teacher to use available resources in creative ways. The availability of technology may allow a teacher to have groups of students work independently. Time is another important consideration in designing a course. How often, how long, and over what period of time will the class meet? How much time is available to the teacher to prepare for the course and the classes? A teacher may adjust her teaching priorities according to the length of the course. The kinds of activities she designs may be affected by the amount of time she has, both in class and before class.

The institutional philosophy, policy, and curriculum are important givens. Having to work within existing curricular guidelines is both a constraint and a resource; so is having to devise one's own syllabus. The type of adminstrative and clerical support provided by the institution affects a teacher's choices. For example, lack of clerical support will suggest streamlining paperwork and materials. Support from the adminstration for innovation will encourage experimentation.

The numbers, levels, and cultural backgrounds of the students are both a constraint and a resource. For example, a large class may cause a teacher to focus on classroom management. A multilevel class may influence the teacher's selection of material or activities.

The teacher herself is the most important given. Her background, experience, and beliefs play a significant role in the choices she makes. For example, one teacher will focus on certain content because she deems it essential to successful language learning, while another will ignore the same content. A teacher who usually develops her own materials may choose to use published materials when teaching a course whose content is new to her.

The givens of a situation cover a broad range of factors and affect every decision a teacher makes. Teachers plan and teach courses not in the abstract but in the concrete of their constraints and resources. For example, an ESL teacher who teaches in an intensive English program, whose students change from one program to the next, may need to investigate the background and proficiency of her students, whereas for a high school EFL teacher, this may be a given because she knows the students. The teacher in the intensive English program might begin with a question such as "How can I find out the cultural background and needs of my students so that I can address those needs effectively in the six weeks of the course?" The high school teacher's initial question might be quite different, say, "How can I keep my students motivated in a required course?" Course development, like teaching, is not a neatly organized process but a complex one in which teachers are constantly considering multiple factors and proceeding on many fronts.

Issues

The givens of one's teaching situation, both tangible and intangible, cannot be ignored. Effecting change requires both recognizing what can be changed and accepting what cannot. The "If only . . ." syndrome (if only we had the technology, if only we had quieter classrooms, if only our students were more motivated) can obstruct change as firmly as the "Yes, but . . . . syndrome (Yes, but that will never work in my setting.) Problematizing enables a teacher to decide what she can change, what she can't, and where to start.

Conclusion

The components discussed in this chapter and summarized in Table 1, should serve not as a checklist for the teacher but rather as a set of tools for talking about, understanding, and directing the process of course development. Each component is contingent on every other component. For example, assessment depends on how one conceptualizes content or on how one interprets students' needs. Conceptualizing content in turn influences the course goals and objectives. Thus wherever one starts in the process, each component will eventually come into play. Each component is, in many respects, one way of working with the whole, as we will see in the following chapters.

References

Auerbach, E. 1993. Putting the *p* back in participatory. *TESOL Quarterly 27* (3): 543–545.

Auerbach, E., and N. Wallerstein. 1987. *ESL for Action: Problem Posing at Work*. Reading, Mass.: Addison-Wesley.

Brindley, G. 1989. The role of needs analysis in adult ESL program design. In R. K. Johnson, ed., *The Second Language Curriculum*, pp. 63–78. Cambridge: Cambridge University Press.

Brinton, D. M., M. A. Snow, and M. B. Wesche. 1989. *Content-based Second Language Instruction.* Rowley, Mass.: Newbury House.

Brown, J. D. 1989. Language program evaluation: A synthesis of existing possibilities. In R. K. Johnson. ed., *The Second Language Curriculum,* pp. 222–243. Cambridge: Cambridge University Press.

California Department of Education. 1993. *English as a Second Language Model Standards for Adult Education.* Sacramento.

Canale, M. 1983. From communicative competence to communicative language pedagogy. In J. Richards and R. Schmidt, eds., *Language and Communication,* pp. 2–27. London: Longman.

Center for Applied Linguistics. (1983). *From the Classroom to the Workplace: Teaching ESL to Adults.* Washington, D.C.

Clark, C., and P. Peterson. 1986. Teachers' thought processes. In M. Wittrock, ed., *Handbook of Research on Teaching,* 3rd ed., pp. 255–297. New York: Macmillan.

Damen, L. 1987. *Culture Learning: The Fifth Dimension in the Language Classroom.* Reading, Mass.: Addison-Wesley.

Das, B. K. 1988. *Materials for Language Learning and Teaching.* Singapore: SEAMEO Regional Language Centre.

Dubin, F., and E. Olshtain. 1986. *Course Design: Developing Programs and Materials for Language Learning.* New York: Cambridge University Press.

Fingeret, A. F. 1993. *It Belongs to Me: A Guide to Portfolio Assessment in Adult Education Programs.* Durham, N.C.: Literacy South.

Gorsuch, G. 1991. Helping students create their own learning goals. *Language Teacher 15* (12): 3, 9.

Grant, S., and L. Shank. 1993. Beyond questionnaires: Engaging learners in needs assessment. Presentation at the TESOL conference, Atlanta.

Halliday, M. A. K. 1973. *Explorations in the Functions of Language.* London: Arnold.

———. 1975. *Learning How to Mean: Explorations in the Development of Language.* London: Arnold.

Hughes, A. 1989. *Testing for Language Teachers.* Cambridge: Cambridge University Press.

Hull, L. 1991. Self-monitoring and self-evaluation: A guide for facilitating independent and autonomous learning. Unpublished master's thesis, School for International Training, Brattleboro, VT.

Hutchinson, T. 1984. *Project English.* Oxford: Oxford University Press.

Hutchinson, T., and A. Waters. 1987. *English for Specific Purposes: A Learning-Centered Approach.* Cambridge: Cambridge University Press.

Hymes, D. 1972. On communicative competence. In J. Pride and J. Holmes, eds., *Sociolinguistics,* pp. 269–293. Harmondsworth, England: Penguin.

Johnson, R. K. ed. 1989. A decision-making framework for the coherent language curriculum. In R. K. Johnson, ed., *The Second Language Curriculum,* pp. 1–23. Cambridge: Cambridge University Press.

Kolb, D. A. 1984. *Experiential Learning.* Englewood Cliffs, N.J.: Prentice Hall.

Kramsch, C. 1993. *Context and Culture in Language Teaching.* Oxford: Oxford University Press.

Larsen-Freeman, D. 1986. *Techniques and Principles in Language Teaching.* Oxford: Oxford University Press.

Low, G. 1989. Appropriate design: The internal organisation of course units. In R. K. Johnson, ed., *The Second Language Curriculum,* pp. 136–154. Cambridge: Cambridge University Press.

Nunan, D. 1985. *Language Teaching Course Design: Trends and Issues.* Adelaide, Australia: National Curriculum Resource Centre.

————. 1988a. *The Learner-Centred Curriculum.* Cambridge: Cambridge University Press.

————. 1988b. *Syllabus Design.* Oxford: Oxford University Press.

————. 1989. *Designing Tasks for the Communicative Classroom.* Cambridge: Cambridge University Press.

Omaggio Hadley, A. C. 1993. *Teaching Language in Context.* Boston: Heinle and Heinle.

O'Malley, J. M., and A. U. Chamot. 1990. *Learning Strategies in Second Language Acquisition.* Cambridge: Cambridge University Press.

Oxford, R. 1990. *Language Learning Strategies: What Every Teacher Should Know.* Rowley, Mass.: Newbury House.

Prabhu, N. S. 1987. *Second Language Pedagogy.* Oxford: Oxford University Press.

Richards, J. 1990. *The Language Teaching Matrix.* New York: Cambridge University Press.

Richards, J., and T. Rodgers. 1986. *Approaches and Methods in Language Teaching.* New York: Cambridge University Press.

Richterich, R. 1980. A model for the definition of language needs of adults. In Trim, Richterich, Van Ek, and Wilkins: 31–62.

Rigg, P. 1989. Language experience approach: Reading naturally. In *When They Don't All Speak English: Integrating the ESL Student into the Regular Classroom.* Chicago: National Council of Teachers of English.

Saphier, J., and R. Gower. 1987. *The Skillful Teacher.* Carlisle, Mass.: Research for Better Teaching.

Savignon, S. 1983. *Communicative Competence: Theory and Practice.* Reading, Mass.: Addison-Wesley.

Shafiqi, I. 1991. Using a student-centered approach to teach grammar. Unpublished master's thesis, School for International Training, Brattleboro, VT.

Stern, H. H. 1992. *Issues and Options in Langue Teaching.* Oxford: Oxford University Press.

Tarone, E., and G. Yule. 1989. *Focus on the Language Learner.* New York: Oxford University Press.

Van Ek, J. A. 1975. *Threshold-level English.* Oxford: Pergamon Press.

White, R. V. 1988. *The ELT Curriculum: Design Innovation and Management.* Oxford: Blackwell.

Wilkins, D. A. 1976. *Notional Syllabuses.* Oxford: Oxford University Press.

3 Designing workplace ESOL courses for Chinese health-care workers at a Boston nursing home

Johan Uvin

Johan Uvin, originally from Belgium, has extensive experience in workplace ESOL with immigrants in the Boston area. He has taught immigrants, worked in staff development, written proposals, and directed workplace literacy programs. He has managed workplace education grants and, since 1993, has supervised adult basic education development efforts for the Massachusetts Department of Education. In this chapter he gives us "a tale of two courses." He designed and taught a course for Chinese health-care workers in Boston using the competency-based methods in widespread use at that time. He spent over ninety hours doing an exhaustive needs analysis that involved not only the students but also nursing staff, supervisors, patients, and administrators. He decided, however, that even though the course did what it was designed to do, it had failed his students. In this chapter, he tells us why he felt this to be the case and how he radically redirected the course as a result.

The course development focus for this chapter is needs assessment. Consider the following questions as you read:

In this account of course development, who determined what the students' needs were? How were those needs defined?

Uvin describes two approaches to course design. In each approach, how were the students involved in determining needs?

In my third year as a teacher at the Chinese-American Civic Association (CACA), we received a grant from the U.S. Department of Education's National Workplace Literacy Program to provide a course for Chinese health-care workers at the South Cove Manor Nursing Home in Boston. I was asked to design the course, which would be taught by me and by my colleagues in two 22-week cycles.

---

1 Portions of this chapter are reprinted from the author's 1991 master's thesis, *Needs Assessment for Workplace ESOL: The Case for Ongoing and Participatory Needs Assessment* (Brattleboro, Vt.: School for International Training), and with permission from Nancy Centrella, Lloyd David, and Johan Uvin, *Teaching and Learning English as a Second Language: Curriculum Resources for Nursing Homes* (Needham, Mass.: Continuing Education Institute/Chinese-American Civic Association, 1992).

Getting started: Collecting information about what is needed

Based on past experiences, CACA had allotted ninety hours for me to collect data and familiarize myself with the nursing home prior to actually writing the course. I spent three weeks familiarizing myself with the goals and processes involved in the delivery of patient care. I worked alongside nursing assistants and got to know the workers who had expressed an interest in the program. I spent time at the nursing station and learned about technical aspects and the language demands of the various jobs. I recorded samples of interactions that workers engaged in. I talked to workers individually and in groups. I spoke with residents. I interviewed supervisors, nurses, and trainers. I attended a training session. I went through a facility orientation. I read the employee manual and looked at training materials. I met with the administrator and her department heads. I tried, through these activities, to solicit the perspectives of workers, supervisors, nurses, residents, and administrators regarding what the course should do to be considered successful.

One of my major tasks was to analyze the jobs of workers by identifying the literacy requirements of the key tasks they needed to accomplish daily and by analyzing the main communicative situations or target situations where workers needed to understand or speak English to get their jobs done. More specifically, I was asked by CACA to list all tasks, break them down into chronological steps, and identify where English was needed most in delivering and documenting restorative care.

The development process: Working with the gathered information

After immersing myself in the nursing home community for about three weeks, I used the information I had collected to create a course outline and to develop units of work. This process consisted of the following steps, which I accomplished before instruction began:

1. Identify the competencies that enable nursing assistants to perform their jobs, focusing on competencies that facilitate direct communication and hence promote the quality of patient care.
2. Develop a test that reveals which competencies workers can perform already and which they cannot perform yet to identify the individual needs of learners.
3. Determine instructional objectives using the test results.
4. Select and sequence the content of instruction:
   – Define the function, setting, interlocutors, register, and medium of the communication for each competency.
   – Select language samples from the initial investigation.

    – Identify grammar points and pronunciation contrasts.
    – Define the cultural information that learners need to acquire.
    – Organize the material from linguistically less to more complicated.
    – Recycle critical language.
5. Write activities to teach to the competencies.
6. Develop materials that facilitate teaching and learning.
7. Design assessment situations to measure achievement and performance objective checklists to document it, specifying the conditions and expected performance level.

The product: Something to teach from

Using this process, I developed sample units of work. Each unit met the following criteria:

- It grouped certain tasks that learners needed to perform on the job.
- It listed the skills that enable learners to perform each task, including listening, speaking, reading, writing, numeracy, and math skills.
- It defined the communicative context of the tasks, specifying the function or purpose, the setting, the interlocutors, the medium, and the register of the communication.
- It provided some language samples and vocabulary.
- It identified grammar points and pronunciation contrasts.
- It gave information about American culture in general and about patient care delivery in particular.
- It suggested activities and resources.
- It ended with a series of assessment activities that teachers could use to measure the attainment of competencies and provided checklists to document achievement.

Following are the units I developed initially, as well as the tasks included in each.

Unit 1: Training for the job
- Introducing self to Staff
- Participating in tour of the facility
- Participating in orientation and on-the-job training

Unit 2: Starting the day
- Getting dressed for work
- Getting to work
- Signing or punching in, reporting to the nursing director
- Relating to staff
- Checking assignments
- Organizing care

Unit 3: Providing daily care
- Waking up residents
- Explaining procedures
- Preparing residents for meals, activities, therapies, visits, and appointments
- Assisting with toileting
- Managing incontinence
- Bathing and shaving
- Dressing and grooming
- Attaching protheses and aids

Unit 4: Transporting residents
- Stating destination of transfer
- Lifting, moving, seating, and positioning residents
- Using the elevator
- Walking with residents

Unit 5: Serving and feeding
- Matching diet cards with trays and ID bracelets
- Describing food to visually impaired residents

Unit 6: Reporting
- Reporting changes in condition
- Measuring and recording intake, output, personal care, and specimen collection
- Measuring and recording vital signs
- Reporting hazardous and emergency situations, accidents, abuse, mistreatment, and neglect

Unit 7: Providing for safety
- Answering call lights
- Applying and releasing restraints
- Documenting restraint release
- Preventing the spread of infection

Unit 8: Promoting comfort and well-being
- Protecting oneself
- Relating to residents
- Relating to visitors

Unit 9: Attending and participating
- Participating in patient care rounds and reviews
- Participating in meetings
- Participating in in-service meetings

The implementation stage: Detecting strengths and weaknesses of my initial course design model

The first 22-week cycle of instruction allowed me to assess the effectiveness of the course I had designed as my colleagues and I were implementing it. We identified both strengths and shortcomings.

STRENGTHS

Once in the classroom, I recognized certain strengths. My course did address competencies that promoted the quality of patient care – the nursing home's basic reason for wanting the program. In addition, the course outline I had produced gave classes direction. Furthermore, the correspondence between the competencies and the language requirements described in the skills section of the National Nursing Assistant Examination was almost one-to-one. Finally, the test scores and performance objectives checklists met the various demands for accountability as expressed by funders, sponsors, and managers.

SHORTCOMINGS

Though funders, sponsors, and nursing home administrators and managers felt comfortable with the mainly work-related focus of the curriculum and its accountability mechanisms, learners expressed several concerns. Through active listening, I was able to identify the following shortcomings of my initial approach.

Content   I had addressed only the work-related needs of learners, and my perception of those needs had guided my initial decision making about what to include or leave out. I learned quickly, however, that learners wanted more than just the language to perform their jobs. As many of the learners in the programs were recent arrivals, they had language needs that went beyond the workplace and so demonstrated resistance, inconsistent attendance being the major one. I had also failed to accommodate the affective, social, cultural, cognitive, and metacognitive needs that learners expressed. I had overlooked the issues posed by entering a new culture, such as culture shock, or loss of social status. Nor did I address skills, strategies, and attitudes that enabled learners to acquire the competencies they needed to develop. For example, many learners did not know how to go about learning a language or used an extremely limited number of learning strategies. Consequently, what they learned was not sustained or internalized. Quite a few learners learned by rote and for the short term only. They memorized the language to describe a tray of food (Unit 5) but failed to recall it or use it freely in the actual communicative context. In designing the course outline, I had also assumed the equality of teaching and learning time, whereas learners, depending on a variety of factors, needed more and varying amounts of time to attain certain competencies than the estimated teaching time I had envisioned.

Methods Content aside, most of the methods I suggested were inappropriate – culturally or personally biased. Initially, much to my surprise, they turned out to be incompatible with the preferred learning styles, strategies, and activities of Asian learners.

The suggested activities also did not facilitate the learning of each individual learner and took for granted that learners knew how to learn. In other words, they were geared toward the educated learner. In fact, some learners had received little or no formal education in their home country, China. Some learners, for example, needed exposure to basic learning strategies such as repetition and substitution.

Another shortcoming was that the teaching activities did not fully take into account the multilevel nature of classes. I also learned that most of the activities I designed were teacher-centered in the sense that they required me to assume the role of the intermediary between learners and the materials, unlike real-life situations, where the learner interacts directly with the material. For example, during several classroom activities, learners were able to read their biweekly assignment sheets with my facilitation. Out on the floors, however, both workers and supervisors reported that the reading of assignment sheets continued to pose problems.

Assessment In addition to the content and methods, the assessment activities in the curriculum were inappropriate as well. They were not always compatible with the assessment needs and preferences of learners. Older learners in particular perceived tests or quizzes as threatening.

As my awareness of shortcomings grew, I became convinced by the end of the first cycle that change was needed for two reasons: Learners did not participate actively in course-related decision making and therefore could not always identify with the suggested content and methods, and I had completed course design and development activities before instruction. The course consequently failed to absorb changes at the nursing home as they occurred or were planned. I concluded that the product I created was unworkable and could not be implemented and replicated with various groups of learners in similar contexts and at various points in time. Rather than trying to fix the product, I decided to involve the people who had a vested interest in the course on an ongoing basis (learners, supervisors, residents, and administrators) in the process of developing a course.

The second approach: A process view of course design

As a result of my evaluation of the first planning and implementation of the course, I realized that I needed to involve the learners at each stage of the process: preplanning, teaching, and assessment or documentation of learning. This process is cyclical and consists of the following stages:

1. Collaborate with learners and facilitate their participation as researchers in the investigation of their daily experiences.
2. Identify issues learners are facing.
3. Find out what needs to be done to resolve the issues we identified, and avoid them in the future.
4. Negotiate with learners as to which activities promote their learning in and outside the classroom, and fine-tune my teaching accordingly.
5. Involve learners in documenting their achievements and in evaluating the process.
6. Develop units or records of work (curriculum products) that account for the work done along the way.

As with the development of the first course, learners were not the sole agents in this process. Residents, trainers, supervisors, and administrators were involved as consultants. They helped us identify and understand the issues the nursing home was facing and provided valuable information about the contexts of the learners' work-related communication needs. They also assisted us in clarifying the link between the nursing home's needs and goals and those of learners.

To find out what the issues were, I began my investigation before instruction started and continued it throughout instruction. During the initial weeks of classes, I focused on the experiences of learners that relate directly to the goals of the program. To be able to identify issues along the way, I established various feedback and input mechanisms.

Investigating the daily work experiences of learners to identify issues

Table 1 shows who was involved in the initial investigation prior to the start of a course. It also lists the various activities used to facilitate it and which decisions were made.

The initial investigation did not necessarily reveal the significant issues in the daily lives of workers. It didn't always enable me clearly to define the needs and goals of learners either. Therefore, I did two things. I established input mechanisms to identify needs and issues along the way, and I facilitated a classroom-based investigation of the daily experiences of workers during the initial weeks of instruction.

Table 1   *Initial investigation*

Activity	Focus of investigation	Decision
Meet with learners individually	Backgrounds Reasons for enrollment Needs, goals, and abilities Availability Preferences: preferred learning arrangement, activities, and assessment instruments Communication issues and barriers	Admit or refer
Meet with residents, supervisors, nurses, department heads, trainers, and administrators	Issues they feel need to be resolved Goals and processes in patient care Language requirements	Negotiate (or renegotiate) goals, design, and logistics Allocate (or reallocate) resources
Meet with learners in a group	Common issues Preferred and favorable learning arrangement Common goals Methodology	Select learning arrangement Scheduling Grouping Consensus on initial teaching 'mode' Select issues
Work with learners	Technical aspects of individual jobs Communication patterns and language use requirements Communication issues Health, safety, and cultural issues	Select written materials that are essential Select issues
Meet with Advisory Board consisting of managers, administrators, supervisors, learners, and program staff	How program goals translated into objectives Evaluation needs and preferences	How assessment and evaluation will be done

Table 2 *In-class investigation*

Topic	Purpose
The Chinese immigrant experience	
Past experiences	To validate experiences
Reasons for immigrating	To build a group
Experiences entering a new culture	To establish trust
	To establish a support network
Histories of Chinese immigrants in the United States	To identify common experiences and issues
History of the Chinese community in Boston	
Support services in the Chinese community	
Daily work experiences of immigrant workers	
Whom workers speak English with, where, how often, about what, and why	To increase self-esteem by identifying where learners use English already
What, when, and why workers read and write at work	To increase the learners' abilities to describe their working environment and their daily work experiences
Roles of individual workers and the role of their departments in patient care	
Working conditions	To identify the learners' understanding of their role in the delivery of patient care
Roles in decision making	
Channels of communication accessible to workers	
Challenges for immigrant workers	
Miscommunications	To identify where English is needed most, analyze challenging interactions (who? where? when? how? about what? why?), and analyze challenging tasks
Recordkeeping	To identify which written materials cause difficulty
Working conditions	To identify health, safety, and cultural issues
Underemployment	To identify barriers to job advancement
Certification	To identify challenges

I established the following input mechanisms to identify issues and needs on an ongoing basis:

- Keeping dialogue journals with learners
- Meeting with supervisory and administrative staff
- Participating in the meetings of the advisory committee
- Establishing classroom rituals (e.g., What happened at work today?)
- Keeping and reviewing learners' work
- Feedback sessions at the end of class
- Planning house visits and field trips in the learners' communities
- Listening actively to learners in class and outside class (e.g., on breaks)
- Spending time in the working environment

Table 2 describes the classroom investigation and its goals.

The following example demonstrates what a classroom-based investigation looks like as it relates to the bottom section of Table 2. It is an assessment of the needs of learners on the basis of interactions they engaged in. Workers were asked to indicate which interactions were difficult and to specify why. A classroom chart of these interactions was made. Here is an uncorrected excerpt from the responses:

What are you doing? Why?
　I am in the dining room take the patients to eat encourage patients.
What are you saying?
　Mary please open your mouth to eat lunch.
What is difficult?
　Patients don't cooperate.

Working with issues and needs

Once I had identified significant themes or issues in the daily work experiences of learners, I worked with them in a variety of ways. I analyzed them. I specified what needed to be done – taught and learned – to resolve them. I implemented activities that enabled learners and me to do so, and we documented outcomes jointly.

Problem posing

One way I used to integrate these tasks was the problem-posing approach (Wallerstein 1983). In this approach, the issue is presented to learners as a problem. Various means can be used to represent the issue, including audio and video recordings, visuals, photographs (e.g., two in contrast), printed text (e.g., dialogues or stories), and skits.

For a representation of an issue to work well, I make sure that learners can recognize the problem immediately, that different aspects of the problem are included, that no solutions to the problem are suggested, that the problem is represented in a nonthreatening way, and that the representation is not overwhelming.

When introducing a problem in class, I go through the following steps:

1. Discussion
   - Describing what happens
   - Defining what the problem is
   - Connecting the problem to the experiences of learners
   - Identifying the causes and consequences of the problem
   - Listing what can be done, drawing from success and failure stories
2. Planning
   - Listing various actions that can be taken to resolve the issue
   - Identifying the resources needed
   - Exploring the consequences of actions
   - Deciding who will do what, when, and why
3. Action
   - Implementing what was planned
   - Practicing what is needed
4. Feedback
   - Identifying what was learned and how
   - Identifying areas for further learning

AN EXAMPLE

From my meetings with supervisors, I identified the following issue. Supervisors pointed out that the use of single-word sentences and the misuse of forms of address upset residents. I wrote two dialogues between a resident and a housekeeper. One dialogue, based on input from the learners, consisted of three lines. The other dialogue was based on the minimal language requirements workers are expected to meet as specified in the skills section of the National Nursing Assistant Examination. By contrasting the two, I was able to present the issue in its complexity without suggesting any solution to resolve it.

1. Dialogue based on National Nursing Assistant Exam language requirements

Jin: Hello, Mr. Smith. Can I come in, please?
Joe: Sure. Come in.
Jin: Mr. Smith. I am Jin. I am your housekeeper today. I'm going to clean your room. Is that OK?
Joe: Go ahead.

Jin: How are you today, Mr. Smith?
Joe: Not too bad. By the way, you can call me Joe.
Jin: OK, Joe. Could you sit on the bed, please, while I clean over here?
Joe: Sure.
Jin: Thanks a lot.
Joe: You're welcome.

2. Dialogue based on learners' input
Joe: What are you doing?
Jin: Clean. You on bed.
Joe: Get outta here! Leave me alone!

We worked with the dialogues in the following way:
1. I read the conversations several times.
2. Learners asked clarification questions about the language used.
3. We discussed the two versions with learners, clarifying why Joe got angry in the second dialogue but not in the first.
4. I made a chart listing for each learner when residents had gotten angry at them and why.
5. Learners wrote about their experiences independently or with the help of a bilingual peer who transcribed verbatim where the interaction took place, when, how often, and why.
6. Learners reenacted the stories of learners, decided how they could change them, rehearsed the changes, and planned to use what they learned on the job.
7. I solicited feedback on the outcomes of the learners' attempts
8. I documented which competencies learners achieved and recorded additional changes in my progress notes.

Other ways

EXPERIENTIAL LEARNING METHODOLOGIES

Problem posing assumes some preinvestigation. Sometimes, however, issues must be resolved immediately. In those cases, experiential learning methodologies (Erkamp 1981) can facilitate a classroom-based course design process. These are the steps that enabled me to integrate course design tasks into the classroom agenda:

1. Learners shared their daily work experiences with one another.
2. Learners compared their experiences and identified similarities and differences.
3. Learners investigated the context of their experiences and identified causes and consequences.

4. Learners identified aspects of their experiences that they wanted to explore further.
5. Learners identified their strengths and weaknesses.
6. Learners and teachers discussed which individual and group activities would enable them to learn what they needed to learn or know.
7. Learners practiced or carried out their assignments.
8. Learners gave, received, and responded to feedback on what they learned and how.

AN EXAMPLE

1. Learners shared their daily work experiences with one another:

   D.T. walked in very upset and told her classmates that she had been hit by a patient.

2. Learners compared their experiences and identified similarities and differences:

   D.T.'s experience triggered many others. An emotional discussion revealed that all workers who worked on the second floor had had similar experiences.

3. Learners investigated the context of their experiences and identified causes and consequences:

   D.T. described what happened, where, when, and why as she saw it. In collaboration with her peers, D.T. described the resident and the room and listed step by step what she and the resident did and said. We acted out the incident twice. During the first reenactment, D.T. participated. During the second one, she stepped back, observed herself, and gave feedback on the accuracy of the reenactment. In a follow-up discussion, learners said that this situation was stressful and that they were scared when assigned to take care of this resident. Some said that they had been seriously injured as well. They said that the resident's abusive behavior was caused by loneliness and depression over a recent stroke. Subsequently, all learners wrote about their experiences with angry residents and developed frequently needed reporting language in doing so.

4. Learners identified aspects of their experiences that they wanted to explore further:

   Learners wanted to know what their own rights and those of the resident were and what they could do or say to protect themselves.

5. Learners identified their strengths and weaknesses:

   Learners knew all the patient's rights. They did not know what their own rights were. All agreed also that they did not know what to do or say in situations like this one.

6. Learners and teachers discussed which individual and group activities would enable them to learn what they needed to learn or know:

> I asked learners if they thought that training would help and if it would be useful if they could know how to ask for training. They didn't think so. Instead two learners wanted to find out more about the patient's condition and decided to ask the charge nurse about it. Three learners wanted to know their rights. I suggested that they read the bilingual nursing home manual and report to class next time. We decided to practice how to ask for emergency help, how to ask the charge nurse for information, and how to put a resident at ease.

7. Learners practiced or carried out their assignments:

> In small groups, learners rewrote the transcript of step 3 as a play. I asked them to include full sentences instead of single words and to think of ways to calm down a resident. They acted it out several times.

8. Learners gave, received, and responded to feedback on what they learned and how:

> I asked learners if and why the play was helpful and what should come next. They said they needed additional practice.

As the example shows, learners do not go through these steps chronologically. They can go through several steps at the same time. Overlap occurs, and very often learners will switch back and forth following the natural flow of the learning process where action and reflection feed into each other constantly.

Strengths and weaknesses

STRENGTHS

As in the first version of the course, learners attained the competencies that are critical to the delivery of patient quality care and certification. However, because they had a say in what was learned, how, and why, their learning went beyond the job-specific competencies. Our collaboration enhanced their sense of ownership, motivation, and self-esteem. Attendance stabilized, and retention improved. The classroom atmosphere became more enjoyable both for learners and teachers and there was a spirit of collaboration and solidarity. Learners also became better language users and learners as they participated actively in the investigation of the contexts where they needed English most and identified all factors that shaped them. Through its responsiveness to learner needs and preferences, classroom activities also became more compatible with the preferred learning activities of learners. Classes were more responsive to the personal, affective, cognitive,

and metacognitive needs of learners. Materials were highly relevant because they stemmed from the workplace or were generated by learners.

WEAKNESSES

Problem posing and experiential learning methodologies do not always
work as a means to make course design an integral part of what is happen-
ing in the classroom, at least not initially. Learners may feel uncomfortable
sharing their experiences at first. They may also feel overwhelmed at first,
and their self-confidence may go down as classes reveal how much they
still need to learn. More important, however, is that learners may not
identify with this approach and may perceive it as inappropriate for a
language class. To overcome these obstacles, I established the necessary
trust and mutual respect first. I explained the purpose of the approach and
gave clear examples that demonstrated that it is possible to learn English by
analyzing one's experiences. I also adjusted my teaching activities to the
preferences of learners.

An ongoing and negotiated or participatory approach to course design
also requires more preparation and follow-up time. This may be an additional drawback unless the working conditions are such that they allow for
this extra time investment.

An additional drawback is that it is virtually impossible in this view of
course design to predict at the onset of the program precisely what the
needs will turn out to be. As funders tend not to commit themselves to a
program or course unless the extent of need has been clearly demonstrated
and documented, this may jeopardize the implementation of a more
dynamic and more participatory approach to course design. Even if learners
are involved in establishing the need for a course and in the initial contract
negotiations, it will still be impossible to set future needs in advance.

Another issue is that to negotiate course content and methods with
learners – particularly beginning ESOL learners – bilingual assistance is
often required for complete effectiveness. In the early stages of our program, this type of assistance was lacking and posed an additional barrier.

What I learned

Finally, I would like to reflect on my experiences and identify what I have
learned about course design as I evolved from a teacher-directed
competency-based system that defined course content and methods a priori
to a more participatory process where I engaged in a process of negotiation
with learners, my ultimate goal being to make courses more worthwhile and
more responsive to learner needs. A key learning point has been that course

design does not take place in a vacuum. Several factors shape the process and directly affect its outcome. Although further investigation is needed, from my experience at the South Cove Manor Nursing Home I have identified the following seven factors as important to acknowledge.

PARTICIPANTS

As when designing any course, I considered the participants. The number of participants informed my decision making. The fact that courses had to serve as many people as possible, for example, directly determined the goals I chose and their achievability.

Several other factors influenced how I went about designing a course. Key personal factors were age, educational and occupational background, mother tongue, motivation, first language literacy, needs, goals, abilities, availability, previous language-learning experience, views of teaching and learning and roles that go hand in hand with them, individual styles and strategies, preferred learning arrangements (such as group versus individual instruction) and activities, and assessment preferences.

Cultural factors also influenced both the process and the product. For participants to identify with the course goals, content, methods, and assessment procedures, I had to acknowledge their cultural expectations. For example, most participants were used to knowing in advance what the course content would be and requested materials for review as well as preview. The commonalities among participants with regard to what a "good" class should look like were also striking and could not be denied to avoid a mismatch between their cultural views and mine.

TEACHER EXPERIENCE AND PHILOSOPHY

The design of a workplace ESOL course also depends on my own experience and values. My beliefs about language, literacy, teaching, learning, and the process of course design — and by extension curriculum development and education — governed my actions and greatly determined how I set goals, selected and sequenced content, designed or chose activities and materials, and specified how assessment was to be done. These beliefs also defined how I viewed the role of the learner, my own role, and, in the case of ESOL courses in the workplace, the roles of supervisors, managers, union officials, sponsors, and funders.

In addition to my beliefs, my knowledge of and skills in course design influenced the process directly and the outcome indirectly. At first I was not adequately trained. I was not formally introduced to what course design entails for workplace ESOL courses to be successful. Over time and as a result of teacher sharing sessions, training, and mentor coaching, my understanding of the course design process became gradually more sophisticated, and my course design skills developed accordingly.

PARTNERS

Besides the experiences and views of learners and myself, I also had to acknowledge the views of more players than is usually the case in designing a course in a more traditional educational setting. Residents, workers, supervisors, nurses, administrators, managers, funders, and sponsors all had agendas. Sometimes these agendas overlapped; at other times, they seemed in conflict. The challenge was to strike a balance between the agendas of these people and mine and to mediate their viewpoints on several occasions.

Closely related to the different agendas were the ranging and fluctuating levels of interest in and support for the program. Depending on a variety of factors (staff changes, personalities, etc.), I could not take ongoing and nursing home–wide commitment and support for granted. When designing a course, therefore, I needed at times to make a conscious effort to strike a balance between the various sources that informed the course design process.

PHYSICAL CONSTRAINTS

Another factor I had to work with was the learning environment. On the one hand, the learning environment at South Cove Manor was not optimal. One classroom was used as a physical therapy room when there were no classes. Another one was so small that certain classroom activities were excluded. It also did not have a chalkboard, and no newsprint could be put up. The noise level in one class was high during the morning tests of the emergency generators located on the classroom's roof. There were also an almost uninterrupted stream of announcements over the paging system, regular fire and evacuation drills, and other distractions.

An additional drawback of the learning environment was the varying amounts and types of English that workers on different floors were exposed to. Whereas workers on the second floor, for example, interacted mostly with English speaking residents and Chinese residents in good mental condition, workers on the third floor had less exposure and fewer opportunities to practice English due to the condition of residents. In designing a course, I had to address these differences in the goals I set and the activities I chose to achieve them.

On the other hand, the learning environment was optimal. I had easy access to human and material resources and, as a result, was able to develop a clear sense of where English was used or not used. In contrast to ESOL programs outside the workplace, I did have the opportunity to examine the context of the learners' needs, to see how their needs and goals related to the nursing home's, and to observe for myself any transfer of classroom learning to the job or to involve supervisors and nurses in doing so.

TIME CONSTRAINTS

In addition to physical constraints, time constraints guided my decision making. Participants felt that four to six hours of instruction per week was manageable and that courses should last no longer than twenty-two weeks. Also, the irregular schedules that go hand in hand with patient care delivery would make attendance irregular. Furthermore, most participants had family responsibilities and pointed out that they could do very little studying at home.

These time-related factors, in addition to time constraints of the grant, guided me in prioritizing goals and in keeping them achievable as well as in sequencing the content.

IMPACT OF FUNDING GUIDELINES

As the project depended largely on external funds to cover the cost of courses, I had to take the funding guidelines into consideration. These guidelines were very specific and addressed several aspects of the program. I had to design my courses within the confines of the federal grant. Courses were funded for one year initially. The project and course goals had to reflect the needs of the workplace. An evaluation plan had to be put into place that would make the achievement of these goals measurable and provide quantitative information not only on learner achievement but also on organizational change in the areas of improved worker productivity, job performance and quality of work, worker attendance, worker safety, and worker retention. Therefore, the grant recommended that the curriculum processes and products (e.g., materials) reflect the needs of the workplace. The grant also dictated the project management structure, which made me accountable to all the members of the partnership: the learning provider who employed me, the management company who operated the nursing home, the nursing home administration, the federal government, and the workers. Needless to say, the impact of these guidelines on course design processes such as needs assessment; the setting of goals; the selection and sequencing of content, activities, and assessment and evaluation procedures; and the development of materials was far-reaching.

POLITICAL, SOCIAL, AND ECONOMIC CLIMATE

The funding guidelines as they applied to the South Cove Manor project established the link between the nursing home's needs and goals and the political, social, and economic needs of the nation as it enters the twenty-first century in general and the situation in the health-care industry in particular. In designing courses, I had to be aware of the implications of these politicial, social, and economic factors.

According to political and business leaders, workplace ESOL and literacy courses should support organizations (businesses, unions) at the local level, and the nation at the global level, in meeting the demands created by a more technically sophisticated manufacturing and service delivery process and restore or enhance their ability to compete. They should also help organizations cope with the implications of recent demographic changes, that is, assist them in upgrading the skills of minorities, immigrants, and refugees who are now making up the labor pool that organizations recruit from to fill entry-level positions.

To do so, a view of course design – and, by extension, curriculum and program design – has been promoted that begins with an analysis of the goals of the organization and defines the needs of learners in relation to the needs of the organization. In this approach, the critical skills or competencies that workers need to develop to meet the demands required by a more competitive manufacturing or service delivery process are identified. Tests are used to determine the discrepancy between the actual skill level of workers and the minimal skill level the organization requires to achieve its newly defined goals and to decide whether a course is necessary. If so, resources are allocated. Instructional goals are set to bridge this gap drawing from the needs assessment. Activities and materials are developed and measures are put into place to assess achievement and evaluate the course. When all these tasks are accomplished, the course is implemented. Initially, I was advised to take these common course design practices into account. My experience has led me to question them.

Conclusion

In this chapter, I have used my experiences with two very different models of course design to identify some key factors that affect the course design process and its outcomes. Course design for ESOL in the workplace is not done in a vacuum. Several factors shape the process, including the participants, the teachers, the partners, the funder, physical constraints, time constraints, the political, social, and economic climate, the specific culture of the workplace, and common course design practices. Both of the models I used had advantages and drawbacks. My experiences, however, have demonstrated the importance of viewing course design as an ongoing process that involves learners actively in identifying course content, methods, and assessment tools.

ANALYSIS AND TASKS

One of the most striking aspects of Uvin's experience is that he followed a seemingly logical set of steps – doing a needs assessment, defining competencies based on the assessment, developing a diagnostic test, determining objectives based on the results of the test, selecting and sequencing the content of the instruction, writing activities, developing materials, and designing assessment tools – but discovered that doing so did not produce a course that he felt worked for his students. The content was too narrow: Although it reflected their working needs, it did not account for cultural and affective needs such as adjusting to a new country or to diminished social status. Moreover, the teaching methods did not match students' expectations and abilities, and so attendance was low. The main problem, as Uvin saw it, was that the course had been designed without student participation, a method of planning he calls a priori design because it was done prior to in-class contact with the students.

There is an apparent contradiction here because the extensive (three week) needs assessment included consultation with the students and even working side by side with them. This situation underscores the fact that a needs assessment is not an objective, context-independent undertaking. It depends on how the analyzer defines (or is asked to define) *needs*. In this case, needs were defined in terms of competencies, the language and behavior necessary to complete given tasks. A competency-based view of needs was the prevailing view in workplace course design at the time and partly an outgrowth of the necessity to document progress and outcomes for funders. This particular course was designed to correspond to a state examination for nursing home workers. Thus the students and their perceptions of their needs were only one part of the process of determining needs.

Uvin made the decision to reorient his course radically so that it would include and respond to input from the students. His rationale for the change was that one syllabus could not serve each group of learners, as both their learning needs and their working conditions would vary. One way to view the shift in approach was that the first approach had presented him with a predefined problem – how to improve the workers' English competence on the job – and a series of steps that would lead to its solution. Teaching the course and observing and listening to his students forced him to problematize his situation: to recognize their dissatisfaction and to figure out ways to meet their needs within the considerable constraints of the situation. He developed a set of steps that included learner involvement at each stage of the process: identifying issues to work on, determining how to address the issues, choosing activity types, developing ways to assess progress and achievement, and producing materials and records of the work done. Because the course content developed as it unfolded and because the learners were involved in its development, he called this new approach a *process* view of course design. Classroom-based investigations and activities for involving students relied on experiential learning and problem-posing techniques, which require students to identify issues of concern, explore the issues with the teacher, and devise ways to address them.

Ironically, Uvin's exhaustive needs analysis in the long run may have given him both the criteria for judging his initial course design as unsatisfactory and the ability to negotiate a syllabus with his students. In other words, he would not have been able to undertake the kind of collaboration and problem-posing activities he describes without an intimate knowledge of the context and the students' trust in him. Furthermore, he was able to gain the continued cooperation and involvement of supervisors and administrators and thus ensure the survival of the course in its new form.

Uvin's narrative highlights questions regarding the extent to which a teacher can be responsive to students' needs. Many, if not most, teachers cannot undertake the kind of comprehensive initial needs analysis Uvin did. Hence determining student needs must become part of classroom instruction time. Many teachers do not have the liberty to negotiate a syllabus with their students but must instead work from an existing one. It is possible to involve students in determining their needs, goals, and preferences as learners, but that takes time. As Uvin points out, it also requires a view of learners as collaborators in a process, a view that many learners may not initially share. Nevertheless, teachers like Uvin show us that it is possible to change one's conception of the role learners play in determining and responding to needs.

FOCUS ON NEEDS ASSESSMENT

1. Freewrite or brainstorm for three minutes in response to this statement: When I think of *students' needs,* I think of . . .
2. Uvin conducted an extensive initial needs assessment. Review page 40 and list the needs assessment activities he did. What kinds of information does each activity provide concerning learners' needs? Which activities are feasible in your context?
3. Uvin changed his course because the learners weren't involved in its development and he felt he was being unresponsive to their needs. His solution was to work in such a way that learners were involved with each step. Review the steps on page 45.

Which steps do you consider to be both feasible and desirable in your context? How would you go about them? List the steps you would like to explore further.

4. In the second (process) view of the course, Uvin conducted precourse and ongoing needs assessment activities.
   a. *Precourse needs assessment.* Review Table 1. In the column headed "Focus of Investigation," which items provide objective data and which provide subjective data; (See page 13 for definitions of objective and subjective data.) Is this distinction useful?

   Which needs assessment activities are feasible in your context? List the ones you consider desirable, and explain why.
   b. *Ongoing needs assessment.* Review the list of input mechanisms on page 48. Which steps or techniques are feasible in your context? List the ones you consider desirable and why.

   Review Table 1. Which activities were designed to build the learners' trust in the process of negotiating a syllabus? List the kinds of activities you consider desirable.
   c. Look over the lists you made for parts (a) and (b), and select three to five activities that you could (or do) undertake in designing your course. Why did you choose these?

5. Uvin felt that the methods he used in his first course did not match his students' expectations of how they would be taught or take into account their learning styles and educational background, what might be called the students' learning needs "what they need to do in order to learn." (see page 15) He included an assessment of their expectations and learning preferences in his second course design. What are your students' expectations of the way they will be taught? Do your methods match these expectations? Give an example of a mismatch (real or hypothetical). How could you resolve such a situation?

6. Review the examples of problem posing and experiential learning techniques on pages 49–52. What do they have in common? How do they involve learners in negotiating the course content? What principles of such techniques could you apply to your context?

7. Review Uvin's wrap-up on pages 54–57. He lists the constraints and resources that he had to take into consideration. Does the list make sense to you? How would you change it to fit your context?

8. *A course outline provides a sense of direction for both teacher and students.*

   A course designed prior to meeting with students will not meet their needs.

   Are these statements contradictory? Can they be reconciled? How? Develop an example based on a course you have taught.

References

Erkamp, A. 1981. *Ervaringsleren* [Experiential Learning]. The Hague: Netherlands: De Hortsink.

Wallerstein, N. 1983. *Language and Culture in Conflict: Problem-Posing for the ESL Classroom.* Reading, Mass.: Addison-Wesley.

4 Designing a seventh-grade social studies course for ESL students at an international school

Pat Fisher

In addition to teaching transition classes for ESL students entering the academic mainstream, Pat Fisher, also teaches English literature and chairs the English Department at an international school in Japan where she has worked for more than a decade. Her department has been instrumental in curriculum development efforts at the school, having piloted different approaches and conducted workshops on the writing process and alternative assessment, such as portfolio use. In this chapter, she describes how she developed an ESL social studies course for seventh graders (middle school). Although the students' needs were clear to her, how to translate those needs into objectives and how to organize the objectives into meaningful, teachable categories constituted a challenge. Meeting the challenge involved hours of studying the objectives and content of ESL and mainstream textbooks and searching for a way to represent the organizing principles of her syllabus graphically. A pie chart proved to be the answer, and its development is described in this chapter.

The course development focus for this chapter is determining goals and objectives. Consider the following questions as you read:

What is the relationship between Fisher's overall goals and the specific objectives?
One of Fisher's main challenges was how to organize the objectives. What helped her to meet this challenge?

"The new 'Freddy' is awesome, man! It's really exciting!" Like all adolescents, my students were reluctant to give up their weekends to return to the classroom that morning. I tried a transition, seeking a connection between their favorite monster and Ghengis Khan, whom we'd started studying the week before. What would happen if Freddy met the Mongol scourge? "Ghengis is tough, man," my best student defended. "The Mongol army was awesome." "What did they do that was so effective?" I asked Hiroshi. "Unh . . . uh . . . uh – they were really good, ya know."

I was back at a familiar place. Did Hiroshi not answer the question because he hadn't understood my earlier explanation, replete with whiteboard diagrams, of Mongol military organization? Had he understood the ideas but lacked the language to restate them? Had he understood my question? My pronunciation? The word *effective*? Had he even been listening?

The frequent visitors to this English-language international school in western Japan would comment on the communicative fluency of this group ("They sound just like native speakers") without realizing what gaps their slang and broad *a*'s masked. The students had reached a high level of communicative competence in elementary school but were now enrolled in an academic program that made different demands on their language. They had been scheduled into grade-level, American mainstream science, math, social studies, and computer sections, but instead of English and a foreign language, they had two sections of ESOL daily. Their problems were the same in all the classes, including science and math. Although they had developed oral fluency in elementary school, they were unable to make the transition to higher-level, more abstract academic work. They had learned to read but had difficulty reading to learn. Simple decoding skills, effective earlier, were of limited use in deciphering complex patterns of information. Although they wrote charmingly about their personal experiences, they could not manipulate facts for an essay question. Exposure to academic language hadn't led to its acquisition.

I wanted – and had obtained authorization – to teach a course that would bridge the gap between what my students could do and what they needed to do. Where to start? I went to conferences. I read. I talked to other teachers. I knew I wanted a content-based ESOL curriculum but could find no existing course design that met my students' particular needs. I designed a course because I had to. Still, the need to create my own course was far more stimulating than frustrating because of fortunate circumstances. A graduate student at the time, I was concerned with finding the match between student needs, teaching styles, and curricular constraints. My "problem" was an opportunity to explore ideas and conduct research and help my students at the same time. I felt qualified to teach both content and language, as I'd had academic training in both English and the social sciences. My administration had not only given me support but also a free hand (which, of course, entailed full responsibility). Resources and materials, within reason, were readily available and I even had adequate time – a year – in which to design and pilot the course.

My first step was to present a proposal (Appendix A) to the administration, stating the rationale and goals for the prospective offering, which I designated an "ESL social studies" course with equal emphasis on language and content. I spent more than twenty hours preparing the proposal, but that initial effort saved tremendous time and energy later. It not only anticipated areas of potential conflict but also helped focus the ideas exploding in my head.

The document was as explicit as I could make it. The first page was in reference to the proposal itself, explaining the purpose of the document ("To make explicit the principles behind the course design and to provide a framework for discussion and action") and the terms of the pilot year. A section describing the students and their language needs followed, with course goals presented in part 3. I then stated the composition and requirements of the class, emphasizing entry and exit criteria (areas of confusion in the past). I compiled a list of available and needed resources for section 4, and included human and physical resources as well as material assets. The fifth section, weighting the different course elements and time needs, was particularly helpful as it forced me to weigh how much time was to be spent in different activities and to decide on the optimal ratio of course components. The proposal ended with an explanation of student evaluation criteria.

As expected, the proposal was accepted. Not only did it serve as a personal catalyst and guide, but it also officially clarified the position of the course within the educational structure. The goals in the project proposal were these:

1. To raise the performance level of students so as to enable them to function successfully in the mainstream academic social studies course.
2. To orient students to the particular skills, vocabulary, and rhetorical styles of the social sciences.
3. To elevate general language skills in both academic and social settings.
4. To utilize the course as fully as possible for future development work of content teaching.

To this point, my formulation of goals had been effective. The goals referred to a clear need and were so admirable as to elicit complete support for my proposal. However, I soon discovered that I couldn't build a course on them because they didn't say anything. What did I mean by "function successfully" in the mainstream class? Obtaining a passing mark? An A letter grade? An improvement of ten points? What were the particular skills, vocabulary, and rhetoric to which I was "orienting" my students? How would I ever know if general language skills had been elevated "in both academic and social settings"? I needed to learn and think a lot more about goals and accountability, so I started reading. I read some books on curriculum design, but most were theoretical and did not seem to fit my situation. The greatest help came from examining actual curricula and the teachers' books accompanying specific texts. I began with TESOL materials but quickly expanded, using everything from kindergarten to geometry resource materials, looking both for ideas and how to organize them. Elementary school language materials were wonderful. Because state school boards require strict adherence to detailed specifications, American language arts programs are accompanied by lengthy lists of objectives – a perfect source for brainstorming.

As I read goals, I noted the ones I liked on individual note cards. After two weeks, I had nearly five hundred – a four-inch stack. The problem was now to sort and organize them. I would sit on the floor, certain that I had finally found the perfect six categories, only to end up with twenty-seven toppling piles. A good goal, so it seemed, was not easily found. A great many were as vague as mine ("To gain understanding of the contributions of literature to individual and group life"). Others were too specific ("to demonstrate the ability to form *r*-controlled vowels correctly"). Some were formed as teaching objectives in one place ("to teach students the sequence of events leading up to World War II"), as learning objectives in another place ("to identify the major events leading up to World War II"), and as content aims in yet another ("to recognize that the terms of the Treaty of Versailles led to the outbreak of World War II"). For example, was "to review the events leading up to World War II" a teaching or a learning objective? Using the Saphier and Gower (1987) categories of objectives, I identified a further variety of aspects: involvement ("to be able to participate actively in group discussion"), activity ("to maintain a personal vocabulary log"), mastery ("to employ the correct form of the fifty most common irregular verbs"), or thinking skills ("to recognize that drafts and revisions are essential components of imaginative composition"). Considering that I was already dealing with two content areas and all four language skills, I needed to find a way to clarify, accommodate, and compare these varying themes.

Many of the goals sounded worthwhile, but when I tried to explain my inspirations to others, they lacked focus. Remembering that Einstein had once said that if you couldn't explain something to a ten-year-old, you didn't understand it, I decided to pull back and clear my head. I played a lot of my favorite blues singer. And took walks. And made lists. And doodled. In the process, I realized I was very strong on certain points. Foremost, I wanted the course to prepare students to succeed in academic content courses. Following a clustering technique learned from the writing process, I wrote "successful academic functioning" in the center of a blank page and drew a circle around it.

At that moment I realized that "success" had to include autonomy (the ability to function independently without outside instruction) as well as competence (sufficient mastery of material to move on to the next level of study), so I revised the circled goal to read "competent autonomous functioning in the mainstream academic classroom."

Another thing I was sure of was that my function as a teacher was quite different from that of my students. This fundamental distinction had often been blurred in my reading, so I felt it necessary to distinguish the two roles visually. I drew two balloons radiating out from the "functioning" circle and labeled them "teaching objectives" and "learning objectives."

From the beginning, the class was founded on both language and content goals, and, to do justice to each, I had to be clear on my focus at each point in the course. Therefore, I drew two more balloons, but because teaching and learning do not have the same relationship as language and content, I made a separate diagram with the two new components emanating from the central goal.

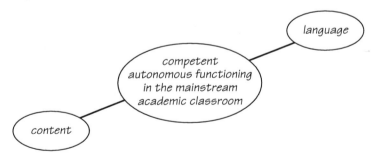

All the while I had been considering the course, I had been thinking about this relationship between language and content. Much of my thinking had been formulated in response to Ana Uhl Chamot and Michael O'Malley's CALLA theory, whose development I had followed since the early 1980s. CALLA, the Cognitive Academic Language Learning Approach, is based on findings in cognitive psychology and concerns how knowledge is acquired, stored and retrieved. Chamot and O'Malley's (1987) research showed that mentally active learners are better learners, which certainly validates classroom teachers' experience. From there, the researchers asserted that different processes and techniques (learning strategies) facilitate learning. Their research centered on academic language learning, which not only employs content-specific vocabulary and discourse features but also requires specialized literacy skills, for example, "Students need to be able to read to learn and to write to express what they're learning" (Chamot 1987: 14). The complexity of the students' task is ameliorated for me by the CALLA assertions that learning strategies can be identified and explicitly taught and that they will transfer to new tasks. I had been informally including what I now realized was learning skills instruction in my classes for several years. That success, plus the research, convinced me that a learning strategies component needed to be presented and taught. A third balloon now radiated from my goal, of equal importance to the course as the language and content elements.

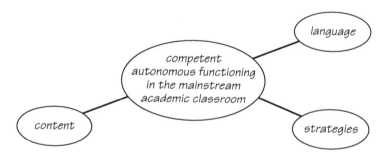

Graphically, I then had two different diagrams, each formed around a center circle labeled "competent autonomous functioning in the mainstream." It was rather like the different wings of a pinwheel, and with that image I knew how to represent the course goals and structure. I placed the diagrams on top of each other, forming a circular graph. Radiating around the common objective was one plane of teaching objectives and a different plane of learning objectives (Figure 1). The learning objectives reflected all three course components, so I refined my teaching aims accordingly. My goal with language was to improve the students' academic language. For competent, autonomous functioning in the content area, I had to teach social studies concepts appropriate to the students' maturational level in their first language. Finally, to ensure competent autonomous functioning, I had to transfer the responsibility for learning from the teacher to the student, which became the strategy aspect of the teaching objectives.

It had taken me one week of immersion in goals, including a few days of brainstorming and ten hours of doodling, to come up with this three-

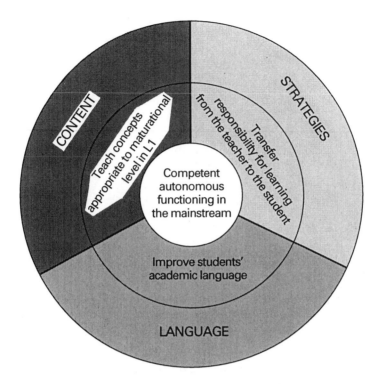

Figure 1

dimensional image of objectives and their relationships, but the remaining course design proved rather pedestrian in execution. Knowing now exactly what I wanted, I could effectively use a textbook I'd already admired. Chamot's *Language Development in Content* series (1987) used a language, content, and strategies approach to teach American social studies to upper elementary and middle school LEP (limited-English-proficiency) students. My students needed more advanced content and language work, but the series was a valuable model. In the accompanying teacher's guide, Chamot (1987) divided the course objectives into awareness and attitude, knowledge, and skills categories, and I adapted these distinctions to elaborate my language, content and strategy goals further. In effect, I added another rim to the circle of my diagram, detailing what was aimed for in the learning objectives (Figure 2). To develop the central goal into a course meant defining what was to be taught, clarifying what was to be learned, and then translating all of it into different types of objectives.

To elaborate the objectives further, I needed another visual model; adding another rim with the index cards would have made a room-size

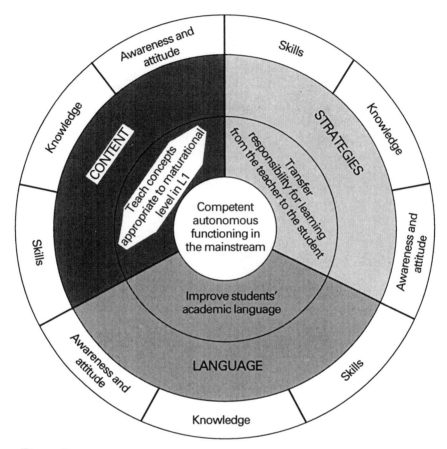

Figure 2

circle. For that next step I adopted the course objectives chart from Chamot's teacher's guide. Her axes were the language, content, and strategy components and the awareness and attitude, knowledge, and skills distinctions. I maintained the relational structures of the circular graph by placing the central goal, teaching, and learning categories to the left of the course components (see Table 1).

This gave me nine categories in which to place my objectives. I went through the index cards again, always referring to my students' needs and abilities and to realistic course parameters. If an objective didn't fit, it was discarded. If it fit but was unteachable in its current form, I revised it. For teaching purposes, the objectives had to be verifiable. "To read maps and graphs with understanding" was a weak objective. "To read maps with demonstrated understanding" was better, and "To read geopolitical maps

Table 1   *Matrix of objectives for the ESL social studies course*

	Teaching objectives		
	Language	*Content*	*Strategies*
Goal:	Improve students' academic language	Teach concepts appropriate to maturational level	Transfer responsibility of learning from teacher to student
Learning objectives: *Awareness and attitude*	By the end of this course, students should be aware that: 1. Different language styles, rhetoric, and vocabulary are suitable to different tasks. 2. Their ability to utilize academic language skills, particularly in reading and writing, will determine their academic successes at Canadian Academy. 3. Language is a source of entertainment and pleasure as well as learning.	By the end of this course, students should be aware that: 1. There are many differences of place, time, and culture in the Eastern Hemisphere. 2. They are each part of a specific place, time, and culture. 3. Environment and lifestyles are rapidly changing in the Eastern Hemisphere. 4. Humankind shares many similarities. 5. There are different ways of satisfying common needs.	By the end of this course, students should be aware that: 1. There is a diversity of learning strategies. 2. The type of strategy used depends on the type of knowledge required. 3. Cognitive strategies can be learned. 4. There is more than one way to accomplish the same task. 5. Others' viewpoints and feelings are worthy of respect.
Knowledge	By the end of this course, students should know: 1. A variety of reading skills and how to direct their reading to a purpose	By the end of this course, students should know: 1. The geographic, topical, and climatic features of the major regions of the Eastern Hemisphere	By the end of this course, students should know: 1. Which learning strategies they use well and which they need to develop

Table 1 *continued*

Language	Content	Strategies
	Teaching objectives	
2. How to write and speak for an audience	2. How geographic, cultural, and historical contexts affect lifestyles and values	2. How to direct their study to a specific end
3. How to process a writing assignment from prewriting through drafting, revising, and editing	3. Of the population explosion occurring in many parts of the Eastern Hemisphere.	3. Which strategy to apply to which task
4. How to present ideas and information orally and in writing	4. What specific problems different parts of the Eastern Hemisphere face	4. How to assess their own studying and work
5. How to use intermediate-level grammar structures correctly.	5. Specific content vocabulary related to proper names, time references, cardinal directions, and key social science terms	5. What to do when they encounter a learning block
6. How to correct such persistent grammar problems as subject-verb agreement, and basic tense errors		6. How to begin and complete tasks in an appropriate time period
7. How to proofread their work for mechanical errors		
8. The vocabulary needed to specify content knowledge and the function words needed to express themselves in the social sciences		

Skill

By the end of this course, students should be able to:

1. Organize, write, and revise sentences, paragraphs, and short essays
2. Write a report to discuss and critique a nonfiction book
3. Write a ten- to fifteen-page research paper containing footnotes and a bibliography
4. Deliver a ten-minute oral presentation with visuals
5. Create a bulletin board display with a short written report
6. Create meaning from context by using context clues and prior knowledge
7. Express both fact and opinion in the content area
8. Summarize and paraphrase information learned from different sources
9. Write using appropriate structures, patterns, vocabulary, and rhetorical devices
10. Explain, give examples, and develop thoughts in reading and writing

By the end of this course, students should be able to:

1. Identify locations in the Eastern Hemisphere
2. Read maps, graphs, and charts with demonstrated understanding
3. Draw maps and charts accurately
4. Read the textbook with understanding
5. Take notes on oral and written presentations
6. Participate effectively in class discussions
7. Follow oral and written directions
8. Take both objective and essay tests
9. Use references to locate information

By the end of this course, students should be able to:

1. Articulate what they are doing on a given task and explain why they are doing it
2. Assess their own and peers' learning effectiveness
3. Plan and build a learning protocol
4. Relate different pieces of information to each other
5. Apply previous knowledge and experience to new situations
6. Determine similarities and differences in data and concepts
7. Manipulate data and concepts in different ways
8. Use other resources
9. Work both independently and in small groups

and circular and bar graphs with demonstrated understanding" was stronger still. All the objectives were also rewritten to ensure uniformity of language. A few weeks' work was all that was needed to organize this information and edit it into final form.

Now the course design was basically complete and ready for implementation. I had put in about six weeks' time, though not continuously, and the spells when ideas were "back-burnering" were probably at least as important as the times spent specifically on task. Once I had formed a clear visualization of the course, the design work went very smoothly.

The course design accommodated itself readily to syllabus implementation. I would read the chapter to be taught in the social studies text, turn to the objectives chart, consider where we were in the scope and sequence of the curriculum, and create lesson plans to meet the varying needs. Having decided the activities for a unit, I would give each student a "contract" listing assignments and due dates (Appendix B). The contract itself enabled students to develop and schedule their own study plans, thus transferring learning responsibility to the students. An activity such as a correction worksheet drawn from student errors (Appendix C) might focus mainly on language objectives, but many assignments covered several objectives. For example, the MAG assignment (Appendix D) – a peer assessment of student-drawn maps – addressed geographic knowledge and map skills (content), spelling and proofreading abilities (language), and task articulation, self-assessment, and small group work (strategies). Others, like the information-sharing lessons (Appendix E), met multiple goals in all three categories. When the school switched texts, a year later, I had only to go back and change some content details, usually to be more explicit.

Since this initial work, I've had to design two other courses, one an intensive English course, one in mainstream social studies. Each took less than a week of work. I worked from the circular graph and the objectives chart, using my own ideas and others' resources to substitute goals appropriate to the new courses. Having already established how I view course elaboration and the relationship of different teaching and learning components, I was confident of how I translated educational ideas into action.

I've learned that several principles work best for me. I need *always* to refer to my students' abilities and needs. I need to be clear on the purpose of the course and the "teachability" of any goal I set. The predesign work is crucial, and time must be allowed for ideas to flow and develop. It helps to listen to music. Or weed the garden. Or walk the dog. Setting forth a clear proposal helps me organize my thoughts and clarifies my working relationships. An image can be worth hundreds of hours of work. And, finally, I've learned, once I'm certain of what I expect from the class, I make my objectives as specific as possible.

Appendix A: Pilot-year proposal

1. *Purpose*

    The purpose of this document is to make explicit the principles behind the course design and to provide a framework for discussion and action. This is a prospective design and therefore subject to change in light of new information or new constraints appearing during the course. Though it is a prospective design, it draws upon research into the needs of ESL students in the content areas.

2. *Students*

    2.1 *Description of students*

    2.2 *Target communication needs*

        2.2.1 Because the Global Studies program demands higher-level reading and writing skills within a social studies context, these skills will be given priority.

        2.2.2 Study skills, such as reading of maps and charts, and research skills will also be given attention.

        2.2.3 Vocabulary needs will be determined by the Global Studies content of the mainstream classes.

        2.2.4 All students in the course require a general elevation of all four language skills and increased fluency.

3. *Course goals*

    3.1 To raise the performance level of students so as to enable them to function successfully in the mainstream Global Studies course.

    3.2 To orient the students to the particular skills, vocabulary and rhetorical styles of the social sciences.

    3.3 To elevate general language skills in both academic and social settings.

    3.4 To utilize the course as fully as possible for future developmental work of content teaching.

        3.4.1 To design a Global Studies curriculum within an ESL context in the middle school.

        3.4.2 To design and pilot instructional materials for said curriculum.

        3.4.3 To evaluate the ESL Global Studies course in light of possible continuation or expansion of content-based instruction for ESL students.

4. *Resources*

    4.1 *Human*

    4.2 *Physical*

    4.3 *Materials*

    4.4 *Course design*

4.4.1 *Student entry criteria*

Appraisal by mainstream content teacher, with consultation of ESL and administrative staff, will initiate recommendation. Scores on standardized tests and in previous classes will also be considered. Final decision rests with administration.

4.4.2 *Student exit criteria*

Student may exit the course and enter the mainstream course provided satisfactory scores have been achieved on mainstream tests, subject to the approval of ESL and Global Studies teaching staff with administrative approval.

4.4.3 *Length*

One academic year

4.4.4 *Intensity*

One class hour per day

4.4.5 *Orientation and Focus*

The main focus will be on developing the language skills required for successful functioning in the mainstream Global Studies 8 course: Reading skills activities will be text-specific and deal with factual comprehension and the ability to form syntheses of what is read. Writing skills will be used to reinforce and extend social studies learning, both of concepts and writing styles, and thus will emphasize chronological and comparison and contrast modes of organization and exposition. Oral expression will generally be in an informal, communicative style, with more formal oral presentations required. Graphics interpretation skills will be integrated within the program.

5. *Components and materials specifications*

5.1 *Ratio of varying components*

5.1.1 Direct teaching of concepts and skills will comprise 25 percent of class time (ten to fifteen minutes daily)

5.1.2 Half of class time will be spent in small group activities involving information sharing, problem solving, worksheet completion, and peer evaluation and correction. Students are expected to use English at all times and to participate actively. During this time, the teacher should circulate and function as coordinator-advisor (twenty to twenty-five minutes daily).

5.1.3 Silent sustained reading should comprise about 20 percent of class time (ten minutes daily).

5.1.4 Approximately 5 percent of class time (one class period approximately every 2–1/2 weeks) will be spent in formal evaluation.

  5.1.5 Students will be given homework assignments two or three times weekly.

 5.2 *Materials*

6. *Evaluation*

 6.1 Students will be required to take the same tests as the mainstream Global Studies 7 students.

 6.2 Students will be required to complete four projects. as are also required by the mainstream Global Studies 7 instructor. These projects will be a book report and a bulletin board display to be completed in the first semester and a speech and a research project to be completed in the second semester.

 6.3 Students will be subject to ongoing evaluation of the activities in 5.1.2, 5.1.5, 6.1, and 6.2.

 6.4 A record will be made of students' present and previous scores on such standardized tools as the IOWA test series.

Appendix B: Student contract

CONTRACT:	Unit Introduction, Chapters 20 and 21 Pages 385–402			
Assignment	Date	Participation	Completion
1. What does the map of Africa tell us?	3/30		
2. Complete outline and write questions	3/31		
3.* Term sheet due	4/1		
4. "Where do I find . . . ?"	4/1		
5. MAG	4/2		
6.* Subheading questions due	4/2		
7. Brainstorming	4/3		
8.* Sentences using ten terms due	4/3		
9. Correction worksheet game	4/6		
10.* Sentence addition paragraphs due	4/7		
11. Which one doesn't belong?	4/7		
12.* Report approval form due	4/7		
13. Lecture and slides, note taking	4/8		
14. TEST REVIEW	4/9		
! ! ! ! ! TEST on Chapters 20 and 21 ! ! ! ! ! FRIDAY, APRIL 10			

Procedure: At the beginning of each unit division, I distribute a contract to each student detailing assignments until the next test. Asterisks mark home assignments. At the beginning of each class, I ask to see the homework assignment, which I either collect or correct in class. The student contracts are marked with my initials and a check, check plus, check minus, or zero, depending on how well the assignment was done. Class participation is marked similarly. Contracts are collected on test days.

Appendix C: Correction worksheet

Procedure: From the beginning of the year, students have worked with correction worksheets containing errors from their own work. Sometimes I collect a variety of errors for the worksheet; sometimes I focus on one item (e.g. subject-verb agreement); sometimes I mix correct and incorrect sentences. The students are always asked to correct the errors, although procedures (individual or pair work, overhead projector, game format, etc.) differ with each assignment. It is important to include work from each student and to type the sheet to preserve anonymity. (However, after a few months, many students are saying things like, "Oh! That's mine – I always forget question marks!") This correction worksheet contains question formation errors that students made while preparing the day 2 homework assignment.

Name _____

ESL Global Studies
Correction Worksheet

Working in pairs, correct the following questions:

1. What is an Artesian spring?
2. From who was the Democratic Republic of Sudan controlled from 1821 to 1955?
3. When did the worst draught occur?
4. What is anthor term for sub-Sahara?
5. Which country have more land than Algeria in Africa?
6. Is Africa the worlds largest continent or the second largest continent in the world?
7. What is the elevation of Sahara desert?
8. How hight do the summer temperaturs go up?
9. Which city does White Nile and Blue Nile join to form the Great Nile?
10. What are most of the surface of the desrt made of?
11. How many main deserts are there in Africa.
12. What do you call people who believes that there are many spiritual forces which rule over nature?
13. What grows in the savana lands?
14. Where is a Nile river located?

Appendix D: MAGs

Procedure: MAGs refers to "map-around groups," adapted from *RAGs,* "read-around groups," a writing process technique (Olson 1987: 148), in which students develop and apply their own criteria to peers' writing or, in this case, maps. With each new country or region, students are required to label and color an outline map. Students work in groups of four to evaluate another group's maps. They have already been trained in constructive monitoring at the early stages. The students generated both the criteria listed below and the scoring procedure of subtracting from a base score of 100.

Map Criteria, ESL Global Studies	
Criteria	Penalty if not met
Accurate location	−5
Requirements met	−5
On-time completion	−5
Neat general appearance	−5
Accurate spelling	−3
Legibility	−3
More than two whiteouts	−3
No wrinkles (one fold allowed)	−3
Same-way coloring	−3
Black felt-tip lettering	−3
Any coloring device except markers	−3
Staying in lines	−3
Bodies of water shown in some way	−3
Land indicated with solid coloring or designs	−3
Lettering style (PARIS or Paris)	−3
Pencil marks	−1
Name	−1
Smudges	−1
Subtracted from a total of 100	

Appendix E: Information sharing

Procedure: In this activity, students cooperate in groups to answer questions based on eight different articles.

> This assignment dealt with endangered species. The students formed groups of four and were given the question worksheet and a packet of four articles. The students discussed the question briefly and assigned the articles among themselves. When all had finished reading their assignments, they took turns sharing their information to answer what they could on the worksheets.
>
> As each group had been given only four of the articles, their answers were incomplete. Each group then sent a reporter to another group to obtain the needed information. Finally, the reporter returned to the original group and reported the answers to the remaining questions.
>
> The articles were from newspapers, reference books, and natural science books taken from the elementary and high school libraries. Because the language in these materials was not controlled in any way, the fourteen questions asked were mainly lower-order and required reading only for specific facts. The difficulty and content of this basic information-sharing activity can be varied according to the materials chosen.

ANALYSIS AND TASKS

The impetus for Fisher's course came from classes she was already teaching. Through contact with her students in those classes, she identified skills they were lacking that they needed to meet the demands of other classes in the curriculum. She asked herself what contributed to the lack of skills, thus searching for what was needed to plug the gaps. Teaching, in effect, was her needs assessment. She felt that the gap "between what my students could do and what they needed to do" could be bridged in a separate course. Her intimate knowledge of her students and the curriculum also guaranteed to some extent that her design could be successfully implemented.

Fisher found that writing a proposal was a way of making concrete the issues that she felt were important in planning the course, both for herself as the course designer and as a way to persuade others of the validity of the course. She tried to be as thorough as possible and to take into account the reality of her institution, such as the resources available and the way the course was linked to the existing curriculum. The issue of entry and exit (passing) criteria was dealt with explicitly, something she hadn't had to do in the past. Also, trying to assign a percentage of time to various components was a way for her to understand what she felt were priorities in the course.

Determining needs, setting goals, and getting the course approved were a fairly smooth part of the process for Fisher. The challenge came when she set about translating her broadly stated goals into a set of concrete subgoals or objectives. As she put it, the goals "didn't say anything" about what or how to teach. This challenge forced her to conceptualize her subject matter – "What do my students need to learn?" – in concrete, teachable ways. Her allies in this process were the available textbooks and her own experience in the two disciplines she was bridging, ESL and social studies, which provided a lens for viewing and selecting from the wealth of published material in social studies. Fisher had a way of making sense of the input, deciding what to keep and what to discard. Also, she did not want to "reinvent the wheel"; if resources were available, she wanted to make use of them.

Fisher found that objectives are written in many different ways, some more useful to her than others. Not only did she have criteria on which to judge the validity of the *content* of the objective, but she also had criteria on which to judge the usefulness of the type and achievability of the objective (Saphier and Gower's [1987] taxonomy.) Thus she learned from both the topic of the objective, and the way it was written.

Fisher's next challenge was to find a way of organizing the mass of objectives she had accumulated. Her first solution was to view the mass of objectives as a self-contained puzzle, amenable to categories that would "use up" all the pieces. If all were valid, all should fit. The key was to find the right way to categorize them. She soon discovered that this was an exercise in manipulation, not organization, because it was no longer grounded in her context. She needed to return to her original conception of the course as the source of inspiration and organization. Fisher realized that if she could put things in the simplest and clearest terms possible, she would have the conceptual framework she needed to organize her material.

Fisher's pinwheel image is striking in that it captures the multidimensionality of the way in which she conceives of the course syllabus and the flexibility of working in a way that is responsive to her students and the material. Her main goal, which is at the center of the pinwheel, is for students to be able to function competently and autonomously in the mainstream classroom. This goal encompasses the three areas of language, content, and strategies. These areas are further elaborated in terms of teaching objectives and learning objectives. For example, with respect to content, the teaching objective is to teach concepts appropriate to the maturational level of the students in their native language. The learning objectives are expressed in terms of developing students' awareness and attitude, knowledge, and skills.

Designing the course enabled Fisher to clarify and make concrete her understanding of theories and models that had appealed to her, such as Chamot and O'Malley's (1987) CALLA model. She, in turn, used the material and models of others in ways that made sense to her. Designating learning strategies as a separate component of her syllabus, one that bridges language and content, demonstrates how beliefs about how students learn influence course design. Fisher's framework, albeit the product of the development of a particular course, nevertheless serves as a framework for other courses she designs because it represents what she believes about what should happen in classrooms.

Finally, Fisher recognized that when engaged in a process like designing a course, one cannot be constantly moving forward and producing results. Taking breaks and finding ways to relax contributed to the success of the course because they allowed her to gain a clear perspective or try a fresh approach.

FOCUS ON DETERMINING GOALS AND OBJECTIVES

1. Imagine that you are explaining the purpose of the course you are designing to someone who knows little or nothing about teaching. How would you explain it? What stands out in your explanation?

2. Write a proposal for your course that takes into account as many of the givens of your situation as possible. Review Fisher's proposal in Appendix A for ideas. Are her categories, (students, course goals, resources, etc.) appropriate for your situation? What categories would you add? Omit? Modify? After drafting the proposal, ask yourself whether it would convince others of the validity of the course. Have you thought of all the possible parameters? Which are most important to you?

3. Review Fisher's goals on page 65. Write two to four goals for your course. Ask yourself these questions: What are my most important considerations in formulating these goals? What are the main purposes of the course?

4. Review the examples of objectives based on Saphier and Gower's taxonomy on pages 18 and 19 in Chapter 2. Write a short list of objectives, related to the goals you wrote for task 3. Then categorize the objectives according to whether they target coverage of content, activity or involvement, mastery, or critical thinking.

5. Review Fisher's pinwheel in Figures 1 and 2. Her three main categories are language, content, and strategies. These categories are further elaborated in terms of teaching objectives and learning objectives. Use Fisher's clustering technique (pages 66–68) to generate your own categories. (You may wish to review "Conceptualizing content" in Chapter 2.) Using the list of objectives generated in task 4, can you arrange the objectives according to your categories? If not, why not?

6. Make a grid. Write the categories you generated in task 5 across the top of a piece of paper. Write "attitude and awareness," "knowledge," and "skills" down the left side of the paper. Write an objective for each category of the grid, using the objectives generated in task 4, if appropriate. (You may wish to refer to Fisher's syllabus in Table 1.) Is the grid useful for you? Why or why not?

7. Find textbooks concerned with the topic of your course. Review the table of contents or proposed objectives. Make a list of the topics and objectives that make sense to you for your course. Go back to your goals or salient points (see task 5) and determine which ones are linked to your conception of the course.

References

Chamot, A. U. 1987. *Teacher's Guide: America: The Early Years, America: After Independence.* Reading, Mass.: Addison-Wesley

Chamot, A. U., and J. M. O'Malley. 1987. The cognitive academic language learning approach: A bridge to the mainstream. *TESOL Quarterly 21* (2): 227–249.

Olson, C. B., ed. 1987. *Practical Ideas for Teaching Writing as a Process.* Sacramento: California Department of Education.

Saphier, J., and R. Gower. 1987. *The Skillful Teacher.* Carlisle, Mass.: Research for Better Teaching.

5 Designing an EAP course for postgraduate students in Ecuador

Maria del Carmen Blyth

Carmen Blyth has taught English as a second and foreign language, developed curricula, and trained teachers in a variety of settings, including Armenia, Egypt, Singapore, and Tanzania. In this chapter, she gives us two avenues into her method of course development. The first is a narrative in the form of journal entries, the second is a series of "mindmaps." Her extensive experience as a teacher and teacher trainer in both EFL and ESL settings had taught her that drawing up mindmaps was an effective way for her to conceptualize the links in the process and to sort out her thoughts and questions. Blyth's prior experience with English for academic purposes (EAP) courses enabled her to do much of the course design before her arrival in Ecuador.

The course development focus for this chapter is conceptualizing content. Consider the following questions as you read:

Why does Blyth conceptualize content as something that students do?
Why does Blyth list what students will do in class without deciding the order in which they will do what and even without having met the students?

This chapter represents a conversation between a teacher of ESL and herself about the process and the product of course design. It is a discussion about issues that a teacher confronts, and the choices she has to make (together with the reasons behind those choices) during the process of designing a course. It conveys the "what" of course design – the actual thoughts that occurs to the teacher as the syllabus takes shape. It also addresses the product of that process and reflects on the circumstances that affect the way the product is interpreted once it has been established and the course is on its way. Finally, it takes a brief look at the factors that should have contributed to the shape of the product, had they been known or believed to be important during the process, but failed to be included.

Vermont, October 10

I just found out that I have secured a teaching internship, a one-month intensive course for adults to be held in Quito, Ecuador, next January. I have no idea at this point what it will involve, but I do have an urge to revisit the world of EFL and adult teaching after six years of teaching ESL to adolescents. Actually, I won't be straying too far from what I have been doing these past six years at the Singapore American High School, as I'll still be teaching English for academic purposes (EAP).

I can't quite envision what it is I am going to do for one hundred hours with the same class. I mean, I can't even begin to plan a course if I don't know what the students are going to have to do in and with the language. If I don't know what the whole point of the course is and where the students stand with respect to that goal, how can I draw up a campaign plan? To be able to plug the gaps means that one has to know what gaps need to be plugged – at least in my book. So I have started drawing up a list (well, more of a mindmap, really) using the information I got from the handout about the program that we were given last week. I am also making notes of any questions that I might have, such as whether final course evaluations are required, and if so, what kind. The answers should give me a better idea of what these people's final destination is (languagewise, that is) and what techniques, activities, and topics might be used to get them there. I think that the program consultant, who is here on campus, will be able to answer most of my questions; if she can't, I shall have to fax the program director in Quito and do a little research of my own.

An afterthought – I wonder what it will be like to have a class of Latin adults again rather than Asian teenagers.

Vermont, November 14

I've been looking at that handout again. On second thought, it really doesn't tell me much, but it is better than nothing. Fortunately, I've been able to pull together quite a few more pieces of useful information, such as the exact aim of the course and who the students are. I'm still waiting to find out the students' particular field of expertise, which should be useful when I finally get to the stage of deciding on a unifying theme for the course and the actual materials to use. Anyway, I feel that I now have enough information to be able to put together the parts of the syllabus that I feel are independent of the individual students involved in the program, namely, the overall course goal and related objectives.

It seems that what I have is a small group of environmentally minded professionals (have to keep that in mind when I start pulling materials), all being funded by the Agency for International Development (AID) to come to the United States to do postgraduate work in their particular field. The course is being run for AID with the sole purpose of preparing these students for that not-too-distant eventuality. So it looks like I'll have them focus on note taking, research skills, paper writing, speedreading, and all the skills associated with such tasks. I am thankful that I have done this sort of thing before – just the mention of EAP triggers thoughts of a whole set of tasks, skills, strategies, and materials that I associate with the field. Now I don't have to start from scratch when designing an EAP course, as I did years ago when I first started teaching in this area. Back then, the "communicative approach" was very much in vogue. I well remember my first assignment in an ESL department in a very British secondary school, when I was handed a *very* functional syllabus (nothing wrong with that if the functions fit the purpose) and told to use it to prepare junior high students in high school academic English. It didn't take me long to figure out that how to open a savings account or confirm a plane reservation was not what these students needed to learn if they were to succeed in a high school social studies or English literature class. It was then that I started to compile my own list of tasks and functions by sitting in on and observing the very classes that my students would be required to take once they had left the ESL program.

I'm also concerned about my students. Because none of them has any experience living or studying in the United States, I wonder if they realize what they're getting themselves into. I assume that they have very little idea of what it means to live on an American campus and take part in what I call the American classroom game. A few *New York Times* articles for both intensive and extensive reading might give them some idea. Considering that they will be arriving in the United States next April to prepare for the August TOEFL, perhaps I had better do some research of my own as to what taking the TOEFL involves and the strategies they will need to get the 550 score required of postgrad students by U.S. universities. Also, when they said that it would be an intensive course, they meant intensive – five hours every day, Monday through Friday, for four weeks straight. We'll all be mental and physical wrecks by the end of the first week if I don't keep them constantly on the ball. I will really have to dig around in my bag of tricks to come up with a well-paced and varied diet of relevant activities!

All these students scored 70 or higher on the Michigan Placement Test. (What might that mean? A little more research for me to do!) I shall have to put them through their paces the first few days and grade the activities according to their capabilities. Anyway, whatever level they turn out to be – advanced, intermediate or beginner – four weeks doesn't seem long enough to help them get their act together for a year of graduate studies in the United States, even if we do have a hundred hours of contact time. It seems to me that I will have to put all my effort into making them aware of where they stand with respect to their language goals and showing them how to make effective use of what they already know and have. I think it would be time well spent if we worked on ways to improve on what they can already do so that when we part company, they can continue to improve on their own if they so wish. In the meantime, I'm making a mindmap to help plan a strategy for teaching the course (Figure 1).

Vermont, December 1

As the start date of my internship approaches, I've been working on that mindmap, trying to clarify things a little. At the start of the map (page 90), I dealt with my reason for finding out why the course was taking place – to determine why this group of professionals would need the language and the context in which the language would be used. This information then determined or prioritized the kinds of discourse and text types that the students would have to be familiar with and the tasks that they would have to be able to do. I came up with such tasks as test taking, speedreading, and researching, which led me to think about what skills we would need to work on if they are to get on the road to becoming autonomous learners. I also started to think of what types of materials I could use with them, such as videos and songs. Then by pulling the skills and the types of materials together, I came up with a list of *possible* techniques and activities I could use – "possible" because I'm sure other factors will come into play when finally deciding on what to use when actually implementing the course on a day-to-day basis, in the lesson-planning stage. Anyway, I feel much better knowing that I've already put together the main part of the syllabus for the course, the part that I consider the stable and staple part, independent of both teacher and students.

Speaking of the lesson-planning stage, I wonder how much of my syllabus I'll have to adjust when I get to Ecuador. That's when I'll have to take into account such factors as the students' backgrounds, individual quirks and idiosyncrasies, and school resources available in order to make the last stages of the syllabus a semisolid campaign plan. For example, the students' ability in the four skills and the type of end-of-course evaluation that will be required of them by AID will together partially determine the types of activities that I use in the classroom and the amount of time I devote to them. In other words, if these students turn out to be quite advanced, as they apparently are, I will probably be doing a fair amount of error analysis and correction with them.

That will help when they take the TOEFL. That test is just full of that kind of stuff, and a five point gain on the Michigan Placement Test is an AID end-of-course requirement.

When choosing activities, another thing I'll have to consider is what exposure (and what type of exposure) to America and Americans the students have already had. I'll also have to look at their own educational backgrounds, EFL included. If they are used to very grammar-oriented

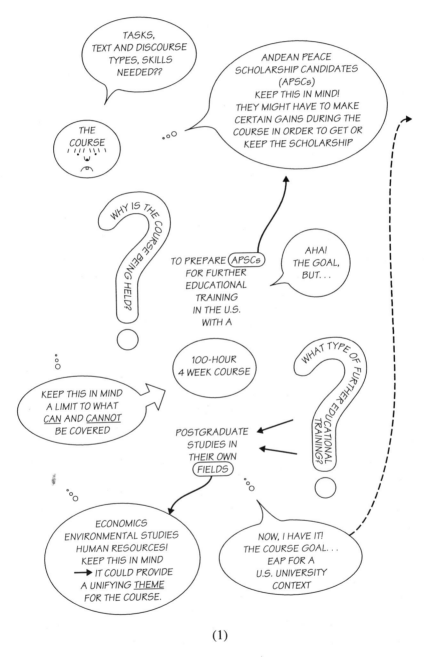

(1)

Figure 1   Mindmap (continues on pages 91–95)

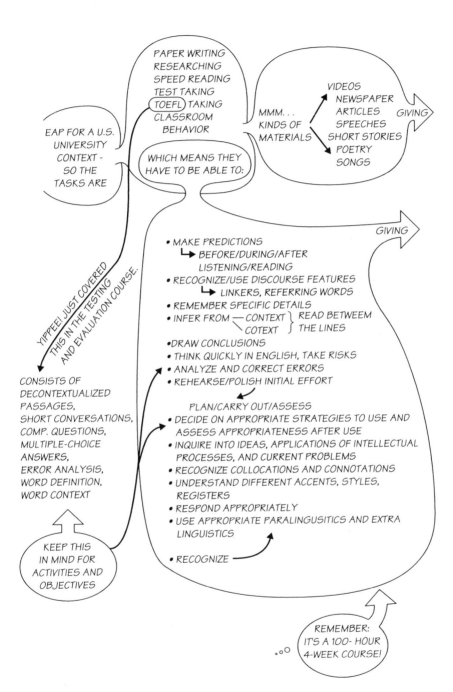

EAP FOR A U.S. UNIVERSITY CONTEXT - SO THE TASKS ARE

PAPER WRITING
RESEARCHING
SPEED READING
TEST TAKING
(TOEFL) TAKING
CLASSROOM
BEHAVIOR

WHICH MEANS THEY HAVE TO BE ABLE TO:

MMM. . . KINDS OF MATERIALS

VIDEOS
NEWSPAPER
ARTICLES
SPEECHES
SHORT STORIES
POETRY
SONGS

GIVING

GIVING

YIPPEE! JUST COVERED THIS IN THE TESTING AND EVALUATION COURSE.

• MAKE PREDICTIONS
  ↳ BEFORE/DURING/AFTER
     LISTENING/READING
• RECOGNIZE/USE DISCOURSE FEATURES
  ↳ LINKERS, REFERRING WORDS
• REMEMBER SPECIFIC DETAILS
• INFER FROM — CONTEXT } READ BETWEEM
               ⟍ COTEXT ∫ THE LINES
• DRAW CONCLUSIONS
• THINK QUICKLY IN ENGLISH, TAKE RISKS
• ANALYZE AND CORRECT ERRORS
• REHEARSE/POLISH INITIAL EFFORT

      PLAN/CARRY OUT/ASSESS
• DECIDE ON APPROPRIATE STRATEGIES TO USE AND
  ASSESS APPROPRIATENESS AFTER USE
• INQUIRE INTO IDEAS, APPLICATIONS OF INTELLECTUAL
  PROCESSES, AND CURRENT PROBLEMS
• RECOGNIZE COLLOCATIONS AND CONNOTATIONS
• UNDERSTAND DIFFERENT ACCENTS, STYLES,
  REGISTERS
• RESPOND APPROPRIATELY
• USE APPROPRIATE PARALINGUSITICS AND EXTRA
  LINGUISTICS

• RECOGNIZE

CONSISTS OF DECONTEXTUALIZED PASSAGES, SHORT CONVERSATIONS, COMP. QUESTIONS, MULTIPLE-CHOICE ANSWERS, ERROR ANALYSIS, WORD DEFINITION, WORD CONTEXT

KEEP THIS IN MIND FOR ACTIVITIES AND OBJECTIVES

REMEMBER: IT'S A 100- HOUR 4-WEEK COURSE!

(2)

ACTIVITIES
AND TECHNIQUES

• ANALYZE A PIECE OF WRITING OR
DISCOURSE FOR TECHNIQUES

TONE, MOOD,
IRONY, HUMOR

• PREACTIVITY
ACTIVITIES → QUESTIONNAIRES,
PERSONALIZED
DISCUSSIONS

DEPENDS
ON HOW
ADVANCED

FIGURATIVE LANGUAGE
PARALLELISM
ALLUSION
ANAPHORA
RHETORICAL QUESTIONS

• STUDENTS PREDICT CONTENT
FROM TITLE OR SUBTITLE
AND QUESTIONS → CHECK TO SEE
IF PREDICTIONS
ARE CORRECT

• STUDENTS DRAW UP A LIST OF
STRATEGIES (EXTENSIVE VS. INTENSIVE)
↳ DECIDE ON WHICH TO USE FOR
INDIVIDUAL PIECES OF READING
AND LISTENING

• STUDENTS FORM OWN
QUESTIONS → PREREADING
PRELISTENING

• STUDENTS PARAPHRASE A PIECE OF A
SHORT STORY OR A SONG

• TEACHER'S → PRETEXT, POSTTEXT.
QUESTIONS   TRUE-FALSE

• INFER OR GUESS ANSWERS TO
QUESTIONS PRIOR TO HEARING OR
SEEING DISCOURSE

• STUDENTS CHOOSE LEXICAL ITEMS
↳ GUESS MEANING
FROM CONTEXT,
CHECK IN DICTIONARIES

• SHORT FILM CLIPS → WITHOUT SOUND, PREDICT CONTENT/LANGUAGE
(PARALINGUISTIC AND EXTRA LINGUISTIC FEATURES)
WITH SOUND, CHECK PREDICTIONS

FAST-FORWARD –
STUDENTS INFER
WHAT HAPPENED
BETWEEN SCENES

STUDENTS PICK OUT IDIOMATIC EXPRESSIONS,
COLLOCATIONS, CONNOTATIONS PREVIOUSLY DISCUSSED

CHECK BY REPLAYING

• STUDENTS ANALYZE, DISCUSS,
AND CORRECT THEIR OWN AND
EACH OTHER'S ERRORS

• JIGSAW < READINGS
LISTENINGS

• STUDENTS LEARN TO GIVE AND
ACCEPT FEEDBACK

• GRAMMATICAL GAP FILLERS
• STUDENTS FREEWRITE TO TEACHER'S
QUESTION (TIME LIMIT)
• 3-, 2-, 1-MINUTE IMPROMPTU TALKS
• 5- to 10-MINUTE PRESENTATIONS
↳ NOTE TAKING
↳ PAPER WRITING
STUDENT GROUPS ↵
REVIEW FIRST DRAFTS
↳ REWRITE SECOND DRAFTS

STUDENTS DRAW UP CRITERIA
FOR GOOD PRESENTATION OR PAPER.
GIVE EXAMPLES OF STRUCTURES,
VOCABULARY, AND USAGE.

(3)

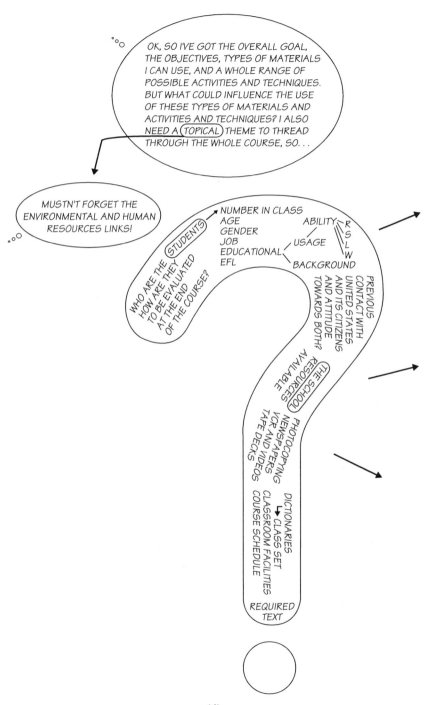

(4)

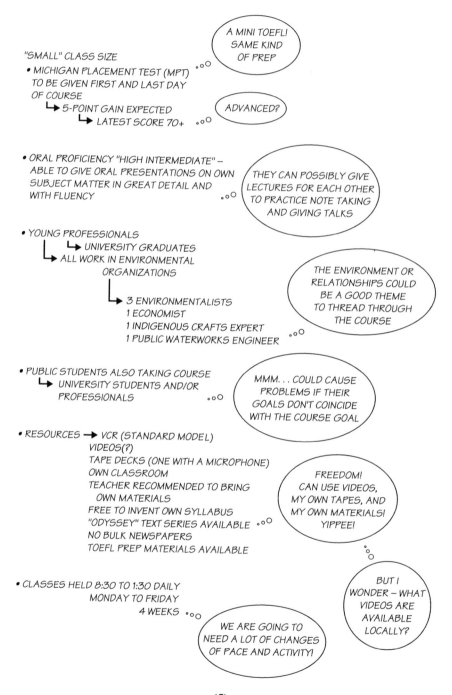

"SMALL" CLASS SIZE
- MICHIGAN PLACEMENT TEST (MPT) TO BE GIVEN FIRST AND LAST DAY OF COURSE
  → 5-POINT GAIN EXPECTED
    → LATEST SCORE 70+

A MINI TOEFL! SAME KIND OF PREP

ADVANCED?

- ORAL PROFICIENCY "HIGH INTERMEDIATE" – ABLE TO GIVE ORAL PRESENTATIONS ON OWN SUBJECT MATTER IN GREAT DETAIL AND WITH FLUENCY

THEY CAN POSSIBLY GIVE LECTURES FOR EACH OTHER TO PRACTICE NOTE TAKING AND GIVING TALKS

- YOUNG PROFESSIONALS
  → UNIVERSITY GRADUATES
  → ALL WORK IN ENVIRONMENTAL ORGANIZATIONS
    → 3 ENVIRONMENTALISTS
      1 ECONOMIST
      1 INDIGENOUS CRAFTS EXPERT
      1 PUBLIC WATERWORKS ENGINEER

THE ENVIRONMENT OR RELATIONSHIPS COULD BE A GOOD THEME TO THREAD THROUGH THE COURSE

- PUBLIC STUDENTS ALSO TAKING COURSE
  → UNIVERSITY STUDENTS AND/OR PROFESSIONALS

MMM. . . COULD CAUSE PROBLEMS IF THEIR GOALS DON'T COINCIDE WITH THE COURSE GOAL

- RESOURCES → VCR (STANDARD MODEL)
  VIDEOS(?)
  TAPE DECKS (ONE WITH A MICROPHONE)
  OWN CLASSROOM
  TEACHER RECOMMENDED TO BRING OWN MATERIALS
  FREE TO INVENT OWN SYLLABUS
  "ODYSSEY" TEXT SERIES AVAILABLE
  NO BULK NEWSPAPERS
  TOEFL PREP MATERIALS AVAILABLE

FREEDOM! CAN USE VIDEOS, MY OWN TAPES, AND MY OWN MATERIALS! YIPPEE!

BUT I WONDER – WHAT VIDEOS ARE AVAILABLE LOCALLY?

- CLASSES HELD 8:30 TO 1:30 DAILY
  MONDAY TO FRIDAY
  4 WEEKS

WE ARE GOING TO NEED A LOT OF CHANGES OF PACE AND ACTIVITY!

(5)

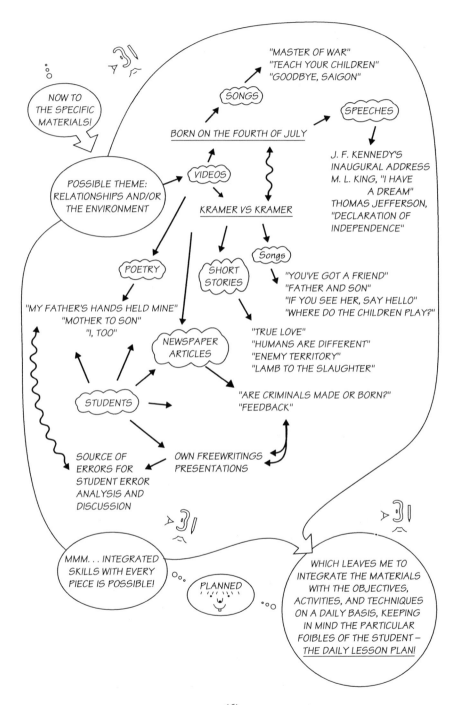

(6)

language lessons, then group and class discussions of discrete grammatical points would be not only appreciated but also valuable. But if their only exposure to the United States has been through movies, then looking at and discussing relevant articles taken from the *New York Times* and the like wouldn't be amiss. I think these two factors, the students' educational background and their exposure to the United States and its citizens, will definitely play a major role in the choice of topics and themes in the materials to be used. However, at this point, I can merely conjecture as to what the individual backgrounds and interests of these students might be, so I can only draw up a tentative list of actual materials to use in class.

Day 1 is most definitely going to be a busy day – not only assessing the students' ability in the language and becoming better acquainted with them but also explaining, clarifying, and, if necessary, discussing how I see the purpose of the course and its objectives. This, for me, seems like the natural place to negotiate the objectives and material content of the course and discuss the techniques and activities I intend to use.

I just remembered something about that Michigan Placement Test score. As a requirement for a course I took this semester, I taught a minicourse to a group of international students who were the same level as the students I'm going to be teaching (70+), and they were at a fairly high level. Now I have some idea about what to expect.

Vermont, 14th December

I just realized that other people might find it difficult to follow my mindmap. I mean, I work well in a nonlinear dimension, but not everybody does. Therefore, I am also making a written copy of the actual syllabus as it now stands (Appendix A). It would make more sense for me to give that to the program director when I arrive in Quito. In the syllabus, I have included a context summary, which gives only information that I consider significant to this particular course – course type, location, students' backgrounds as they relate to the course goal, and curriculum type. For the content section, I decided to stress the types of materials to be used and the tasks they would be used for. When I got to the objectives section, it seemed that the logical place to start was with the students' ability to anticipate form, content, and meaning, as I believe that this ability is fundamental to understanding and responding appropriately on any level. Therefore, my first objective is to develop the students' ability to predict, or at least to narrow down the possibilities of what might be coming next, based on what they already know and what they are able to glean from the whole context. The other objectives logically follow from this ability in that the students will have to be able to identify main ideas, recognize specific details, understand the relationship between main ideas and their expansion, follow a sequence, and infer from context to draw conclusions and act on those conclusions. At the same time, they must be able to recognize the sender's purpose and attitude if they are to act or interact appropriately. It would then seem logical for them to have a means of checking and clarifying information when confusion or uncertainty arises, whether that confusion be caused by an inability to pick out the relevant or significant ideas; to handle varieties of accent, register, style, or different or unfamiliar discourse types and features; or even to communicate effectively. (This also includes a need for students to be able to identify and correct their own errors in form, meaning, or use.) By developing the students' confidence in being able to do all these things they will be able to participate more effectively in inquiries of ideas and current problems. I refer to developing confidence in these skills because I feel that, given these students' educational backgrounds, age, and level in the English language, they will already possess these skills to some degree. Engaging in inquiries of ideas and applications of intellectual processes will allow them to develop their ability to make informed choices and in so doing permit them to reflect on the consequences of those choices. Ideally, in the end they will be able to think quickly and accurately in English and in so doing act appropriately in any given context – or at least have the confidence to take a calculated risk.

I tried to be as specific as possible in the layout of the goal and the objectives to make it easy for the program director to follow. I put two columns under objectives. The left column contains the objectives that need to be worked on; the right indicates ways of reaching those objectives. On my mindmap, I have left off the section with the actual materials to be used, as that will be very much determined by what's available on-site and the interests of the students.

Quito, 19th December

Well, I finally made it to Quito. This morning I met with one of the two program directors (the other one doesn't get back till the first day of the course), and he gave me a tentative class list, tentative because they still don't know how many public students there will be. As of yesterday, there were six scholarship students and five public students. He showed me my classroom, which is pretty small and cramped for a class of eleven or more students, and informed me that he would be unavailable for most of the course. Apparently, he's going to be busy with the General International Meeting (GIM) of the Experiment in International Living, which is to be held in Quito. Two thousand North Americans will be flying in to spend a couple of weeks together, discussing ecological and environmental problems. This would be an *excellent* opportunity for my students not only to be exposed to North Americans en masse but also to exchange ideas with them. There will also be panel discussions, in English, on the problems facing Ecuador at this point in time – a great chance for the students to practice note taking and listening for specific information. The director said that he would see if we would be able to take part in a few of these morning sessions.

The director also presented me with the course syllabus, which was divided into sections on such aspects as grammar, functions, communicative competencies, and topics, none of which I felt could be mixed and matched. I presented him with my syllabus and told him that I would rather work from that. He approved the proposal but said that five hours of TOEFL preparation per week was required. I replied that that was fine by me, as I had already planned for that in my course design. I also discovered that there were no videos available at the school, so I had to join the video club around the corner to get some. It looks as though I will be using the movie *Tequila Sunrise,* at least for the first day, as *Kramer vs. Kramer* is not available. I am hoping to pick up *Revenge* (with Kevin Costner) the first week of the course and plan on using it instead of *Tequila Sunrise* because I think the theme, which deals with the relationship between a Mexican and a North American, is perfect for the course. At the moment it's unavailable, but should be back in the shop by the third day of the course.

Quito, 6th January

I just got back from an orientation session. The director gave us some kind of student evaluation sheet that we are supposed to fill in at the end of the course that specifies areas of improvement and areas that still need work (Appendix B). It seems a little subjective to me. We were also told that the students are used to a very traditional teaching situation, with the teacher being the only voice of authority in the classroom and controlling the students at all times. They are not used to group and pair work, and the use of such techniques would probably lead to complaints. I replied that I was in the habit of explaining to my students exactly why we were doing an activity and how it related to the goal and objectives of the course and had never had any students complain about the types of activities or techniques I used. The director gave me a kind of "don't say I didn't warn you" look and left it at that. He also commented that the students might resent the fact that I was British and not American. I pointed out that even if I were American, it would be no guarantee that they'd be able to understand Americans when they reached the United States, due to the enormous variation in American accents.

I spent the rest of the day planning and photocopying for my first class tomorrow. I made enough copies of the course goal and objectives (the same ones I gave the director) to give to the students on Monday, so they can at least see where I think we need to be going. Then the floor will be open for them to give me their opinions on my course proposal and, if necessary, for me to clarify any areas of uncertainty or misunderstanding. It will also be a good time for them to make suggestions as to the objectives and content of the course, as I've always found it not only interesting but also useful to get the students' perspective and, if appropriate, to integrate their ideas with mine. As usual, I'll also give them a brief description of my teaching experience. That should at least make them more amenable to giving me the benefit of the doubt regarding the techniques and activities I choose.

Quito, 2nd February

I'm almost feeling guilty for not having written, but I've hardly had time, what with planning and teaching five-hour-long classes. Anyway, yesterday was the last day of the course, and I must admit to having been rather sad at saying goodbye to the group. I couldn't have asked for a better class, so I am feeling a little bit down now.

Basically, I was happy with how my syllabus plan went. When I look at the actual course content, (Appendix C) though, I realize how much the course seemed to take on a life of its own once a topical theme was established in my mind. The course seemed to flow quite naturally from one skill to the next, integrating tasks, skills, activities, and topics as it went along and providing variety in both pace and activity. It therefore turned out to be pretty easy to pick and choose from among the tasks, skills, and techniques and activities sections on the mindmaps, which needed to be worked on and matched with the materials available. I was sure glad I brought along all those short stories, songs, and articles. For me, though, one of the most fascinating things was to watch the growing awareness in the students of what it meant to learn and how they, too, could be autonomous learners.

I *was* allowed to take my class to a morning session of the GIM. That proved to be a great success with the students, as it turned out to be a panel discussion on the political and socioeconomic problems facing Ecuador today. The panel consisted of five Ecuadorian experts who each gave presentations (in extremely good English) to the virtually all-American audience and then answered questions from the floor. It was quite an inspiration to the class to see non-native speakers handling a native speaker audience so effectively and confidently. As a matter of fact, when I was asked if any of my students would be willing to take part in the evening open panel session, four of them volunteered. It turned out to be one of the highlights of the course, for they had the opportunity not only to interact with U.S. citizens on a professional level but also to have their abilities tested to the limit. It was moving to note their self-confidence when spontaneously answering questions from the floor or consulting among themselves on a question when necessary. One of the older students told me after the session that it had forced him actually to *think* in English for the first time in his life.

As for my syllabus, it was interesting to note that not only did we cover the grammatical territory mapped out in the prescribed syllabus that the director had given me more than amply, but we also managed to touch on quite a few of the functions outlined. I was concerned that we didn't even skim through the topical and communicative competency sections. However, on taking a second look at them this evening, I can see why – they were just not relevant to the course goal or the participants' needs.

In retrospect, I wouldn't change anything in that original syllabus if I had to do it over again. And from the final written and oral feedback I got from the students, they thought likewise (see Appendix D). However, there are a few things that I would place more weight on. For example, I think that I would try to fit in more actual practice sessions with the TOEFL (but then, you can only fit so much into one hundred hours) and try to emphasize more to the students that they have to realize the strategies available to them and recognize how their choice of strategy influences the outcome. I also think it would probably have been a good idea to have the students keep strategy journals for themselves as well as for me. That may be water under the bridge for this course, but it is something to keep in mind for the next EAP course I have to plan.

I've also noticed that putting or pulling a syllabus together seems to be the act of identifying and separating out the variables from the nonvariables and taking what is stable as the heart of the course. That is not to say that a syllabus is an inflexible instrument, set in stone. However, it should reflect the needs, as defined by the course goal. That way, the integrity of the course can be maintained, irrespective of the instructor teaching it. However, the syllabus must not be so narrowly defined as to disregard the individuality of both teacher and students. For it is in the individual teacher's ability to read the students and interpret the syllabus in accordance with their best interests that a syllabus is realized. That, in the final analysis, is what a syllabus is for.

Appendix A: Preliminary course syllabus

Course Syllabus

Context summary

- EAP at AECIE in Quito, Ecuador
- Ecuadorians, young, graduate professionals from differing ethnic, socio-economic, regional, and professional backgrounds. AID mission scholarship candidates, highly motivated.
- Students will be coming to the United States this year to take the TOEFL prior to starting postgraduate work at American universities. On their return, they will be required to lead community workshops in their field of study.
- Advanced level (70+ MPT). Required to make a five-point gain on the MPT by the end of the four-week, hundred-hour course.
- Teacher free to invent curriculum

Content
Movies, newspaper articles, literature, music, and art (cartoons) that focus on the American way of life
Tasks appropriate to academic English: note taking, research skills, paper-writing, test taking
Practice sessions with TOEFL tests, looking at specific test strategies

Rationale
Students must be able to handle academic English at the graduate level and interact appropriately with American peers and instructors. They must also obtain the score required by American universities on the TOEFL. Furthermore, they will need the skills and strategies necessary to function in everyday American society.
Students must be sufficiently competent in the English language for the cited purposes to function autonomously in an American university context.

Backbone
Thematic: relationships from an American perspective, at an international and national level. How accurately do the media and the arts put this across to non-Americans?

Goal: To develop in students the skills and awareness necessary to function as autonomous learners in the American university context.

Objectives: To develop student self-confidence in the following abilities.

Ability	*Demonstrated means*
To anticipate both form and content	Making predictions before and during reading or listening
To identify the main ideas and recognize specific details	
To recognize the relationship between main ideas and their expansion (examples, etc.) follow a sequence	Recognizing discourse features linkers and referring words such as *he, it, she,* and *which*
To infer from context and cotext (read between the lines)	Understanding organization (introductions, development, etc.)
To draw conclusions	
To recognize the speaker's or writer's purpose (e.g., to ridicule, to amuse) and attitude (e.g., serious)	Recognizing collocations and connotations; comparing discourses
To interact appropriately (e.g., interrupt, reply, question) in spoken and written form	Using appropriate paralinguistics
To seek clarification/check information	
To deal with various accents, registers, and discourse features	Understanding and responding appropriately
To identify and correct errors in form, meaning, and usage	
To rehearse and polish initial efforts	
To inquire into ideas, applications of intellectual processes, and current problems	
To make informed choices in carrying out an activity and to reflect on the consequences of those choices	
To think quickly in English and even take risks	

Possible Techniques and Activities

Reading

Students predict content from title or subtitles then do an initial scan to see if predictions are correct.

Teacher asks questions: Preactivity questions, postactivity questions, true-false questions.

Students individually choose words they do not know. Individuals, groups, or pairs deduce meaning from context and check in dictionary.

Video

Students view short film clip without sound and interpret attitude and purpose of speakers; they then view with sound to check predictions.

Students view short film clip and predict what happened before or what happens next; then they view previous or following scene.

Students keep a journal as if they were one of the characters in the film or give advice to characters; then they view film to check predictions.

Speaking

Students do consecutive three, two, or one-minute impromptu talks on a topic chosen from a teacher- or student-generated list of possibles. Students draw up criteria for a good presentation.

Students and teacher prepare and give five- to ten-minute presentations. Order of presenters and areas to be focused on during class decided on by students.

Writing

Students freewrite for a preset time in response to a teacher question.

Students write papers based on notes taken during a presentation by a native speaker. Students draw up criteria for a good piece of writing.

Students revise first draft and write a second draft. Students analyse or discuss their own and one another's errors. They choose which errors they want to look at.

Students analyze a piece of discourse for techniques. Possible areas of focus: allusion, parallelism, anaphora, figurative language, rhetorical questions, tone and mood, irony, humor.

Listening and reading

Students draw up a list of reading and listening strategies (extensive versus intensive) and select most appropriate. Students conduct post reading and listening assessment.

Students form their own questions according to what they would like to know from the discourse.

Students do jigsaw reading and listening, using paraphrasing and inference.

Student and teacher goals and needs

Teacher discusses her perspective on the course, its goals and objectives, and its rationale.

Students discuss areas for improvement and their motives for taking the course.

Students complete motivational activities such as questionnaires, person-
alised discussions, and use of visuals.
Students and teacher decide on content of the course or the next session.
Students give written and oral feedback on each session periodically and at
the end of the course.

Possible Lesson Plans (days 1 and 2)

WEEK 1:

Day 1

Introductions and questions by
students and teacher.

Discussion of what students see
as areas for improvement and
reasons why they are taking the
course. Teacher's perspective
on the course.

Michigan placement test and sentence completion test administered for listening ability.

Short film clip from *Kramer v
Kramer* (burnt-toast scene),
played without sound, to provide the arena for discussion
and diagnosis. Students build
up a dialogue (in pairs or
groups) for the clip. Replay
with sound to compare and
contrast with their own version
(students write down
differences and similarities).

Freewriting (5 min.) nonstop to
answer the question "What do
you think would happen next in
Ecuador and in the United
States?"

Discussion of test results with students in individual sessions.

Day 2

Discussion of test results with students in individual sessions.

Jigsaw reading "Enemy Territory"
for assessment of critical thinking skills and use of effective
reading strategies, predicting,
inferring, paraphrasing, vocabulary guessing, and expansion.

Informal oral feedback about how
the course is going for students
so far and reasons why.

Presentation and assessment. Students draw up individual sets of
criteria for a good oral presentation and then listen to an
American guest speaker who
discusses how the media por-
tray family life and relationships in the United States and
contrasts those portrayals with
"real life" experienced first
hand. Students take notes during the talk and are allowed to
ask questions at the end of the
talk. Students assess in writing
the speaker's effectiveness
using their own list of criteria.

Homework: Students use notes to
write a paper.

Appendix B: School evaluation form

Student Evaluation

Name _____   Days absent: _____

Date: _____   Days tardy: _____

Level: _____   Total hours: _____

Course dates: _____

Teacher: _____

Please score the student's ability based on the following scale:
(1) Poor
(2) Below average
(3) Average
(4) Above average
(5) Excellent

Circle 1–5 based on the student's ability at your class level:
(1) Poor
(2) Below average
(3) Average
(4) Above average
(5) Excellent

LINGUISTIC ABILITY

Language Proficiency (15)
1. Grammar _____
2. Vocabulary _____
3. Pronunciation _____
Total: _____

Communicative Ability (15)
1. Fluency (speed) _____
2. Comprehension ability _____
3. Ability to express oneself

_____

Total _____

PERSONAL PERFORMANCE

Effort (25)
1. Attendance _____
2. Participation _____
3. Homework _____
4. Motivation (attitude toward learning) _____
5. Ability to progress _____
Total _____

TOTAL SCORE
Linguistic Ability: _____
Personal Performance: _____

FINAL TEST SCORE: _____
(if applicable)

COMMENTS AND RECOMMENDATIONS

MPT SCORE: _____

Appendix C: Syllabus for EAP course as actually taught

Monday	Tuesday	Wednesday	Thursday	Friday
Week 1				
Introductions and questions by students and teacher.	Discussion of test results with students in individual sessions (continued from yesterday).	Organizing: Students write up list of topics.	Students decide on order of presenters, areas to be focused on for feedback, and when the feedback is to be given.	Student presentation (as on Thursday).
Discussion of what students see as areas for improvement and reasons why they are taking the course. Teacher's perspective on the course.	Jigsaw reading "True Love" for assessment of critical thinking skills and use of effective reading strategies, predicting, inferring, paraphrasing, vocabulary guessing, and expansion.	Focus on vocabulary guessing, confirming or correcting guesses with dictionaries + vocabulary expansion.	Presentations: two students give presentations, followed by a question-and-answer session and feedback discussion. Introduce the idea of mindmapping for taking notes during presentations.	Song: "Father and Son." Students in groups look at half the song and decide who the conversation is between and what is being said. Groups tell each other in their own words what their half of the song says and compare the relationship with that of the poem.
MPT and sentence completion test for listening ability.	Informal oral feedback using questions on the board.	In groups, reading and revising first drafts, focusing comments on criteria set by class (coherence, fluidity, organization, grammar, vocabulary and structure) and including a final positive comment (35 min.).	Presentation: Student gives presentation while others take notes for feedback and for information.	Student presentation.
Short film clip from *Tequila Sunrise* (first restaurant scene) (played without sound) to provide the arena for discussion and diagnosis. Students build up a dialogue (in pairs or groups) for the clip. Replay with sound to compare and contrast with their own version (students write down differences and similarities).	Freewriting: "The Age of Technology: Positive and Negative Aspects" (7 min.)	Short clip from *Revenge* Cochran's arrival at the Mendez house; (10 min.), played without sound, to provide the arena for discussion and diagnosis. Students use paralinguistic and extralinguistic features to determine the relationship between the characters.	Follow-up: Half the students write up the information notes while the other half correct mistakes pulled from yesterday's freewriting. Students then change roles.	Short clip (next 10-min. sequence) from *Revenge* to confirm or correct predictions on relationships, plus vocabulary expansion. Continue running vocabulary list.
Freewriting (5 min.) non-stop to answer the question "What do you	Students use freewriting to write a first draft			Incorporate pronunciation focus on problem areas from running vocabulary list and start filling in the Underhill phonemic chart.
	Impromptu speaking: presentations (3, 2, 1 min.) in pairs with feedback from each new partner after each presentation, using the same topic. Before			Student presentation.

think would happen next in Ecuador and in the United States?"

Discussion of test results with students in individual sessions.

presentations students draw up individual sets of criteria for a good oral presentation and then listen to each other. Students take notes during the talk and are allowed to ask questions at the end of the talk. Students assess in writing the speaker's effectiveness using their own list of criteria.

Short story sequencing: "Humans Are Different." Students in groups sequence the short story paragraphs and paraphrase it. Students choose five words from the story they don't know, underline them, and guess the meanings from context and cotext.

Homework: Draw up a list of five topics you would like to discuss in class.

Revisions: Students finish group revisions of first drafts (35 min.)

Creation of a running vocabulary list based on film.

Poem: "My Father's Hands Held Mine." Students sequence the poem and answer questions: Is the writer a man or a woman? Who are the three relatives mentioned? Which culture is the writer from? Give reasons. Give the poem a title.

Teacher reads poem aloud to confirm sequence and discuss variations. Class feedback on answers to questions.

Freewriting: "Is what the writer says true for you? Why or why not?"

Homework: 1. Prepare a 10- to 15-min. presentation on the topic of your choice, taking into account the list of topics drawn up by the other students and hence their areas of interest.
2. Write a second draft of the paper on technology.

Homework: 1. Write up one of the talks you heard today using your notes.
2. Start a journal on reflections on friendships. The journal entries will be looked at in two weeks time.

(Students are given the option to re-present their talks next week.)

Appendix C: continued

Monday	Tuesday	Wednesday	Thursday	Friday
Week 2				
Student presentation. Group work on the articles. Students generate variations on one sentence by the addition or omission of the definite article and explain to other groups. Student presentation. Continuation of work on articles. Explanation of the independent research project. Students will form "expert groups" depending on their area of expertise and inclination to look into how best to distribute a $1 million loan to the small village of Carmen, Ecuador. Students are responsible for organising themselves into appropriate groups and dividing the	GIM panel discussion on Ecuador. Areas of discussion by panel: politics and democracy in Ecuador; economic problems and trends; women in Ecuador; 500 years of resistance. Students take notes and later exchange notes with another student. Students do a write-up from the other student's notes as homework. Individual feedback sessions with students.	As students walk in, get them working on error sheets in groups and rotating from sheet to sheet – each sheet has five sentences with errors in them grouped according to the error and a title giving a clue as to the areas with errors (tense, subject-verb agreement, etc.). Song "Masters of War" for decoding, recoding, inferring and vocabulary extension. Divide class into four groups. Each group gets one piece of the song and tries to answer the questions on the board: Who is the writer talking about? What does the writer think of the person or persons? What is the situation referred to?	Students pick one of their present and one of their past *if* sentences and write them up. Each student explains the two sentences (self-correction, class correction, explanation) and the situations for those sentences. Students then check their other *if* sentences before handing them in. *Listening*: "Understanding TOEFL." Three sections. Side A: Discuss and explain what it consists of, what to listen for, and how to choose the answer. Play three sections. Students discuss in pairs how they decided on their answers. Class as a whole goes through answers. Student presentation.	Focus on vocabulary from the song. Students go through vocabulary together and expand. Feedback article. Students answer the questions on the feedback article from their own experience and discuss answers in pairs. Class feedback on board. Group revisions of first draft on GIM panel discussion (35 min.). Short clip from *Revenge* + freewriting (10 min.) on the question "Do you think Mendez's wife is telling the truth? Why or why not?" Feedback article jigsaw reading. Do first stage of jigsaw. Finish revision of first drafts.

assignment among themselves. Expert groups will be expected to present the last week of the course.

Explanation of task for tomorrow at the GIM: taking notes on the panel discussion.

Student presentation.

Homework: Write down questions you would like me to focus on in our individual feedback sessions.

Reassign into three new groups of four to exchange information. Class feedback to board. Write the name *Bob Dylan* on the board and discuss what the situation was. Class discussion of song. Play song for students to identify their part. Hand out copies of whole song. Play song again.

Talk by Dr. McCormick with question-and-answer session on university life in the United States.

Student presentation.

Homework: 1. Write three sentences with *if* in the present tense and three sentences with *if* in the past tense.
2. Pick five words or phrases from the song that you don't know and guess the meanings.
3. Bring in your GIM paper for group revision Friday.

Homework: Write a second draft.

Appendix C: continued

Monday	Tuesday	Wednesday	Thursday	Friday
Week 3				
Error sheets: As students walk in start work on three error sheets in groups, moving from sheet to sheet (errors taken from freewriting on video clip). Give freewriting back, students identify their sentence or phrase and explain to the class what they really meant for final self or group correction.	Focus on vocabulary: phrasal verbs and idioms from the song and their explanations. For homework, students choose three of the phrasal verbs, write a sentence using each one, and be prepared to explain the context it would be used in and what it would mean.	Writing: Students write up and explain (check verbs: transitive versus intransitive, separable versus nonseparable) for class check and revision.	Return of second draft on GIM. Students choose two or three mistakes they want class input on – students write on board and group corrects.	Return of last freewriting on the video clip.
		Discussion on homework question. Put ideas generated on board. Go into two poems, "Mother to Son" and "I, Too." In two groups, students separate and sequence the two poems and paraphrase them. Vocabulary extension and expansion.	TOEFL preparation: "Understanding TOEFL." Discuss and explain what sections 2 and 3 consist of. Do section 2.	Freewriting: "What circumstances and actions would, in your estimation, prove that someone is a friend?" Students discuss in pairs – feedback to the board.
Jigsaw reading: Finish jigsaw reading on feedback, regrouping for sharing information (recoding and encoding). Feedback to teacher and board. Comparison with prereading answers to questions.	Discussion: On the board, write *Martin Luther King, Jr.*, and elicit what students know about him. Write *I have a dream.* Have students freewrite for 6 min. on their dreams for the future and then share their writing with a partner. In groups of four, brainstorm King's dreams – feedback to board. Hand out text of King's speech and have students find and underline the points from		Poems: three students read aloud and explain their poems.	Hand out words to the song (second verse onward)" You've Got a Friend." Students compare with their composite list and fill in the blanks (inference). Feedback to board. Students listen to the song and check for missing words. Listen to first verse as group dictation. Feedback to board. Listen again to recheck certain words.
			Discussion of answers to section 2.	
Short clip from *Revenge*. Focus on prediction and inference using paralinguistics and extralinguistics.		Clip: last part of *Revenge*. Focus on listening (word boundaries). Freewriting to answer questions: "What is your final opinion of Cochran, the wife, and Mendez? What could Cochran have done differently that might have had different consequences?"	Teacher poem.	
			Completion of section 3.	
			Poems: three students read aloud and explain their poems.	
			Answers to section 3.	Short story: "Lamb to the Slaughter." Jigsaw reading for prediction, inference, and critical thinking skills.
			Poems: students write up their poems.	

Discussion of what constitutes a psychopathic personality and whether a criminal is made or born. Give out first page of *New York Times* article "Are Criminals Made or Born?" Students read to answer the question. Give out second page – timed speedreading using first and last sentences of each paragraph to get a summary. Repeat process with third and fourth pages.

Structured feedback session using these questions: What have I learned these last three weeks? What has puzzled me? What have I enjoyed, hated, and accomplished so far? How have I been learning? What do I want to work on in the final week?

Homework: Take the "Self-defense and Violence Quiz."

Impromptu speaking on minitopics for 3, 2, or 1 min. (as in week 1).

Homework: "Find a poem in Spanish or English that you like and want to read aloud and explain it to the rest of the class."

Vocabulary expansion and free writing: "What is your opinion of Cochran, the wife, and Mendez? Give reasons for your answers."

Song: "If You See Her, Say Hello." Prediction and inference from the title: How many people are involved? What is the relationship between them? Half the class get first half of the song and the other half the second part. Groups work on paraphrasing and filling in the missing words (prepositions). Students pair up and explain their half of the song. Play song for check.

the board in one color and other points in a different color (skimming and scanning). (Play a Koko Taylor tape during the reading.)

Focus on vocabulary in groups and guessing meanings. Each group puts up three items and guesses. Other groups check and correct.

Video: On board, write "What advice would you give Cochran?" Class discussion; put ideas generated on board. Show clip up of Cochran and wife leaving for the cabin. Ask, "What do you think Mendez is going to do?" Discuss question and show next part of video.

Homework: "Do you think Dr. King's dreams have come true in the present-day United States? Why/why not?"

Appendix C: continued

Monday	Tuesday	Wednesday	Thursday	Friday
Week 4				
Kennedy's inaugural address: Use for work on prediction, inference, context and cotext, parallelism, anaphora, allusion (as impact devices). Students skim for gist and analyze for these concerns.	Mock TOEFL.	Focus on error analysis and correction in groups.	Declaration of Independence: Students skim for gist. Focus in on techniques used – parallelism, allusions, rhetorical questions. Compare and contrast with Kennedy's speech.	Predicting. Write the title of the short story "Silent Spring" on three pieces of paper. As they walk in, students write predictions and questions for the story. Divide class into groups and give each group the story cut into paragraphs. Ask them to sequence it and then answer their own questions (analysis and synthesis). Meanwhile, give students individual feedback on their progress. Discuss the fable and the techniques
Video clip of Kennedy's address "Let every nation know" sequence taken from *Born on the Fourth of July*. Students write short speech addressed to the young, attempting to persuade them to act on a social responsibility		Research project on 'La Carmen' – presentations, class feedback, and discussion as to what needs to go into the written proposal.	Impromptu speaking on minitopics for 3, 2, or 1 min. (as in week 1).	
		Clip from *Born on the Fourth of July* (Marine and soda fountain sequence). Freewriting: "What values are portrayed as important by the sequences? How are they similar to or different from your own?"	Short clip from *Born on the Fourth of July* (next two sequences). Focus on word boundaries and vocabulary extension.	

(incorporating the techniques of parallelism, etc.; 15 min.) Students exchange papers and read and decide if they were persuaded or not.

Distribution of final feedback sheets, to be completed and handed in the next day.

used (irony and hyperbole). Students pick out examples of each from the story.

Michigan Placement Test.

Song: "Where Do the Children Play?" Students paraphrase the first verse. Second verse used as a dictation. Third verse given to other class for information gap activity with the two classes. Both classes listen to whole song.

Collect final feedback sheets and "friendship diaries."

Appendix D: Course evaluations

Name: _____

ESL Intensive Course Evaluation

The goal of the course has been to help you develop language-learning strategies and to improve your skills in using the English language with regard to academics. In pursuing this goal, we have worked on the following matters:

1. Critical thinking (jigsaw readings, sequencing poems, etc.)
2. Building vocabulary
3. Grammar
4. Preparing and presenting a talk
5. Taking notes and writing a paper
6. Revising a first draft and writing a second draft
7. Awareness (giving and receiving feedback)
8. Developing a deeper sense of responsibility for your own learning
9. Pronunciation
10. Taking tests
11. Freewriting (thinking quickly in English)
12. Error analysis and correction

Please take a little time to think and write out your responses to the following questions.

1. What has been most useful for you in this course?

2. What would you suggest your instructor continue to do as a teacher of ESL? What would you suggest she do differently?

3. What do you feel you have accomplished in this intensive course over the past four weeks?

4. What do you feel you need now to go one step higher and further in your studies of English?

_____

A SAMPLE OF STUDENT RESPONSES

1. What has been most useful for you in this course?
   The way I learn to "learn" English.

Note taking and writing a paper, first and second draft.
Keeping and increasing my vocabulary.
Error analysis and correction.
Pronunciation.
Developing a deeper sense of responsibility for my own learning.
Being able to speak and read in an impromptu manner.
The video helped me hear and understand dialogues and how Americans act and make a conversation.

2. What would you suggest your instructor continue to do as a teacher of ESL? What would you suggest she do differently?

   I suggest the instructor continue doing the same as in the course, changing the activities, putting special attention on the areas the students need, taking time with each area of language.
   Your form of teaching is the best I know. All the activities you prepare and the manner you lead the class are done to maintain us thinking, writing, and listening all the time in English.

3. What do you feel you have accomplished in this intensive course over the past four weeks?

   I have learned to take responsibility for my own learning.
   I learned a better way to take notes efficiently.
   I am very happy with freewriting because to write and write allowed me to think in English and express my feelings.
   I have accomplished a good way to study by myself.
   I can make my opinions and tell other people.
   Now I am not tied to the dictionary. I am able to read and understand without a dictionary.
   I got to think in English. I think, speak, write, and organize my ideas in English as suddenly as I need.
   I have learned to use Spanish as a tool for looking for new words in English.
   I have learned to catch words and meanings in videos.
   I have learned to take out in a few minutes the main ideas of articles and read fast.

4. What do you feel you need now to go one step higher and further in your studies of English?

   I must speak more in order to improve.
   I think I have to improve my grammar. I think I can improve it by doing some freewriting by myself and then correcting the mistakes.
   I need to listen to videos and tapes.
   I have to learn not to feel uncomfortable with interrupting someone.
   I think I have to read more. I have to learn to use words like moreover *and* furthermore *and understand when I use them and what they mean.*

ANALYSIS AND TASKS

Blyth's method of planning involves drawing up "mindmaps," which help her conceptualize and plan the course, its purpose and content, and the applicable constraints and resources. They enable her to define and elaborate the various components and to see them in relation to one another. They give overall order to the process and couch it in an internal dialogue. The maps become menus of purposeful possibilities from which she and the students will draw once the course is under way. They allow her to be prepared but also flexible and responsive to her students.

Blyth's first concern is the purpose of the course, which for her is directly linked to what the students are going to have to do in and with the language once the course is over. Blyth conceptualizes content in terms of doing: what students will do (tasks) in the context and the skills needed to do the tasks. The context includes the discourse and text types that the students will encounter. Her goals and objectives are thus framed in terms of tasks and skills. From past experience, she has rejected a syllabus whose content is function-based as inappropriate for teaching students academic skills.

Blyth's needs assessment and syllabus design (in the sense of deciding what to teach, although not necessarily in what order) are done in the absence of students. She feels that she can determine their target needs both on the basis of her experience with teaching and planning such courses and her experience in an academic setting. The course has the dual purpose of helping students develop the skills needed for the tasks she identifies and of developing confidence in those skills. Confidence building translates into making students aware of what they already know how to do, how they can build on what they already know, and how they can expand their ability to learn independently. Her decision to have students work on "how to learn" is partly the result of a constraint: the course is so short that for them to reach the goal, they may have to continue to work on their own once the course is over.

Materials are an important initial consideration. Once the skills have been identified, Blyth lists possible materials to use. Activities and techniques are related to the skills on the one hand and to the materials on the other.

Blyth identifies her main challenges as how to unify the course thematically while varying the pace and type of activities. She does not decide in advance what will be taught and when. That will be decided once she has met the students. Thus who the students are becomes important once the course is under way. Their backgrounds, interests, and levels will help determine the choice and use of materials. Blyth will explain her rationale for the goals, objectives, and way of teaching. She will seek their input and adjust the course accordingly.

How the students will be evaluated at the end of the course influences Blyth's choice of materials and activities. The students are expected to make a certain gain on a posttest, so Blyth includes activities geared to the test as part of her syllabus. There is an interesting contrast between the course evaluation Blyth gives her students at the end of the course (Appendix D) and the student evaluation she is given by the administration (Appendix B). Her course evaluation asks students to list specific areas of learning and progress. Their answers are expressed largely in terms of what they have learned how to do or what they have learned about how to learn, both of which correspond to Blyth's objectives for the course. The evaluation of students, on the other hand, is concerned with global assessment of students' general linguistic and communicative competence.

Blyth's planning process demonstrates the close links among the various aspects of course development. For example, her students' needs are interpreted as tasks and skills, which are in turn interpreted as content. The selection of materials is dependent on how they will enable students to carry out the skill-building activities. Assessment of learning is done on the basis of what skills students have developed. In some senses, each process is another way of viewing the whole.

FOCUS ON CONCEPTUALIZING CONTENT

1. Review mindmaps 1 and 2, in which Blyth sets out the goal of the course and conceptualizes its content.
   - How does Blyth define the goal for the course?
   - Blyth's point of departure in conceptualizing content is what she calls "tasks" – for example, writing papers. What is the relationship between the tasks and the goal of the course? How are the tasks similar to "target needs" (see page 15)?
   - The tasks in turn suggest both skills and materials. Blyth has listed the skills as objectives such as "Students have to be able to make predictions." What is the relationship among skills, tasks, and materials?
   - For your own course, can you conceptualize content in terms of tasks? If not, why not? If so, make list of contexts in which your students will use English. Choose one of the contexts and make a map or a list of three of the tasks that your students will or may undertake in those contexts and the discourse or text types that they will encounter. Finally, list some related skills and materials.

2. Review mindmap 3, in which Blyth draws up a menu of activities and techniques.
   - How do the activities and techniques relate to the skills and materials?
   - Make a map of some of activities and techniques appropriate for your course.
   - What provides coherence to the activities and techniques?
3. Review mindmaps 4 and 5, in which Blyth lists the constraints and resources of the course, including information about the students. What possible effects do the constraints and resources – for example, the job background of the students – have on Blyth's choice of content?
4. Review mindmap 6, in which Blyth lists the materials she may use, depending on the theme she chooses.
   - How are the specific materials related to the constraints and resources on Map 5, and to the activities and techniques listed on map 3?
   - Are the activities and techniques you generated in response to question 2 feasible within the constraints and resources of your context?
5. Review the mindmap again. Choose an aspect of mapping the course in this way that appeals to you. Make a visual of that aspect for your course (for example, defining and linking the components; posing and answering questions regarding the course; putting together menus of possibilities for one aspect of the course; listing possible constraints and resources). Note that mindmaps are individual and that you should experiment to find the kind of map that works for you. Blyth's original mindmap was not as ordered and neat as the version that appears here.
6. Consider the first day of class. How will you introduce your objectives and way of working to the class? What will you do on the first day to set the tone of the course?

6 Designing a writing component for teen courses at a Brazilian language institute

Maria Estela Pinheiro Franco

In this chapter, Maria Estela Pinheiro Franco, a teacher with more than twenty years' experience in EFL and elementary education, describes the development of a writing supplement to be used in conjunction with the regular courses for teens and preteens at the language institute where she is a branch supervisor in São Paulo, Brazil. Pinheiro started out as a kindergarden and primary school teacher. She then went on to open her own language school, which she ran for five years. She joined Associação Alumni in 1983, first as a teacher and later as supervisor of the teen and preteen programs. Pinheiro draws on her knowledge of her adolescent students, her understanding of materials development, and her experience with writing as a process to produce the writing supplement. Because teacher development is one of her responsibilities as a course supervisor, one aspect of course development she describes is training other teachers to use the material. The Appendix contains all of the material used in the writing supplement for the Teen 6 level. [Note that the space for students to write has been condensed.]

The course development focuses for this chapter are: selecting and developing materials and activities, and organization of materials and content. Consider the following questions as you read:

What were Pinheiro's main considerations in developing the writing supplement?

What factors does she take into account in deciding how to organize and sequence the activities?

Associação Alumni is a large private educational institute that offers EFL (English as a foreign language) courses in São Paulo, Brazil. In my second year as teen and preteen course supervisor, it was decided that a writing component should be added to the teen and preteen courses. At that time I was working with Luciane Nunes, who was the department coordinator. My responsibilities included both teaching and course development. Both of us agreed that our students couldn't write well, even though our first impression was just the opposite: When they got here for the placement test, they usually did much better in writing than in speaking. The reason for the better results was that most of them had had some English at their own primary and secondary schools, where written English and grammar were given greater emphasis. However, as soon as they started taking EFL classes at Alumni, they developed their spoken language more, which is one of the main reasons students take our courses: They want to learn how to speak English.

Alumni has always focused primarily on the teaching of a language as a means of oral communication – listening and speaking skills, with secondary emphasis on reading and writing skills. Our basic course teaches the students how to be appropriate and accurate speakers. However, in addition to evaluating our students' speaking skills, we also evaluate their writing ability through quizzes and written exams. The results of these evaluations were not encouraging. Whenever the teen and preteen students wrote a letter, a description, or a narrative, most would get lost. They were much more successful at dialogue completion exercises, where they had to work with functions and forms previously worked with in class. Their compositions were not always coherent, and it was hard for them to organize their ideas. They also lacked vocabulary and had difficulty describing, defining, explaining, and paraphrasing their ideas and points of view. It became clear to us that we could not expect them to present good results in writing if we were not preparing them to do so. Something had to be done to overcome this problem. It was then that we decided to develop the writing activities.

There were other reasons for including writing instruction in the teen courses. The written language is also used for communication. Our students, for the most part, come from well-to-do socioeconomic backgrounds, and so they travel a lot, make new friends, and often need the written language for correspondence. Besides that, our students would be better prepared for the intermediate course, which follows the basic course and emphasizes the reading and writing skills. Teaching writing would also enable our students to have a better knowledge and awareness of the new language they were using: The students have time to think about the language when they are writing. Writing reinforces listening and speaking, and very commonly, students feel more confident when they are dealing with the written language, for they don't feel as greatly exposed to their peers.

The basic course for which we would be writing the supplement consists of two courses, one for preteens and one for teens (Table 1). The preteen course for 10- to 12-year-olds, consists of six levels. Each level meets twice a week for one hour. The nine-level teen-course for 13- to 16-year-olds, meets twice a week for one hour for levels 1–6, and for two hours for levels 7–9. The students have to complete these nine stages to be able to go on to the intermediate course. The task of designing a writing supplement for the basic course was no small undertaking, but despite the challenge, Luciane and I felt ready for it.

Our first step was to seek approval from the general coordinator of the Deparment of English. Before speaking to her, we analyzed and discussed

Table 1   *The basic course*

Preteen course (ages 10 to 12)			Teen course (ages 13 to 16)		
Level	Class length	Sessions	Level	Class length	Sessions
1 through 6	1 hour	2 per week	1 through 6	1 hour	2 per week
			7 through 9	2 hours	2 per week
			(After Level 9, students may enter the intermediate course)		

the situation in which the supplementary material would be inserted. We wrote a proposal in which we outlined consideration of the following three factors: our students, our already structured course, and the activities that would be added. The school was very enthusiastic about our proposal, for it fit in with the progressive atmosphere of an association that is constantly improving as well as updating its courses. Our proposal was accepted, and we were free to create.

We decided to start with the highest two levels of the teen course, levels 8 and 9, because at that time we were piloting new books for those levels and so would be able to add the new activities as part of the pilot. We decided to create three or four writing activities per level, which would give our students experience in the various aspects of the process of writing and would develop their writing skills for the intermediate course. We knew exactly the kinds of writing we wanted to include, although we were not sure about the nature of the activities. I was the one responsible for creating them.

My first questions in designing the activities were about the students. Who are our teen students? What are they like? I would say that they are very energetic, active, and dynamic, while at the same time they lack confidence and concentration. They spend half their day writing at their own schools, and when they get to Alumni, they are very tired. Besides this, they are usually lazy about writing, and they seem not to see any immediate objective for writing in English. I wondered how to motivate them.

For example, how could I motivate teenagers to be interested in writing a description? What do they like describing? Having recently returned from a trip, I had some promotional brochures about the places I had visited. I decided to try out a sequence of activities based on this material. I brought the brochures to class and asked my students to read them. Then they chose a place they would like to visit and explained their reasons. They were supposed to use the adjectives and expressions they had found most convincing. Their task was to report their choice to their peers and try to convince them that their choice was the best place for them to visit. After that, they wrote their own brochure. At home, they chose a picture of a place they would like to visit and described it using as many of the adjectives and expressions they had seen in class as they could. I was very happy to see that my students were involved in the activities and had fun writing the description of a place they would like to go on their next vacation.

This example illustrates how I created the activities. The first time around was like walking on a path for the first time; the second time, it was much easier, for I knew what to expect and what to do. It took my colleagues and me a year to pilot the writing activities for Teens 8 and 9. Meanwhile, we started thinking about the other levels. We decided to start the writing component in Teen 4 because the students at this level would be better prepared for such activities, having already had three semesters of EFL classes, and they were more mature. Based on our experience with levels 8 and 9, we decided to add four short activities, not linked to the textbook or topics presented, because it would be difficult for us to fit them into an already structured course. Besides, we were much more concerned about our students' likes and interests and so felt that the activities should be linked to our students' reality and needs. Because we teach eight units a semester, one writing activity would be given during the time two units were taught.

As I began developing the activities for the remaining levels, the question of motivation continued to play a central role. My task was to decide what students needed to learn, what kind of input the teacher would give, and what activities the students would do for each level. Many times I had observed that my students would not complain about having to write if they were to fill in the blanks of a song or if they were involved in any kind of group work where they were competing or playing a game. They liked activities where there was a sense of discovery and challenge involved. They liked task-based activities that gave them a reason, a purpose for writing. It seemed to me, then, that the activities would need to have a purpose and be enjoyable or challenging in order to motivate the students. Such activities might include writing a postcard to a friend, a greeting card to a parent, a letter asking for information about an EFL course in the United States, a letter describing what they are like and what they look like, a narrative of a frightening or exciting experience, a description of a place they would like to visit, or an argumentative essay about a controversial topic. All these activities would bring the written English language close to their reality and needs.

I decided to put these ideas together into the four different kinds of writing that were already being taught in the basic course for adults: narrative, description, argumentation, and a diary (journal).

I then had to decide how to divide the types of writing among the six levels and how to sequence the activities within levels. I wanted the students to start with shorter and easier activities and gradually move on to longer and more difficult essays. The activities were grouped in such a way that the initial activities in a level would be more linked to real facts while at the other end students would be freer to create. I also distributed them within levels, taking the categories into consideration. In Teen 6, for example, I wanted the students to work with description and narrative types of writing, and I thought that they would like to describe an object they were fond of and later describe a person they liked very much. A way of introducing a narrative that was close to their reality would be starting their own timeline; besides being a narrative of their own lives, it is something they are used to doing in their history classes. This way they would be learning how to put events in chronological order, which is essential in a narrative. After that, they would tell an anecdote in narrative form. (Teen 6 writing activities are detailed in Appendix C.) I followed a similar organization across levels. Teen 4 students would write paragraph-size writings, whereas Teen 9 students would write composition-size descriptions or narratives. The lower levels would concentrate on narrative and description, and the higher levels would include comparison and argumentation.

I presented the following plan to Luciane:

Teen 4   Error correction exercise
          1. Writing a greeting card
          2. Writing a paragraph
          3. Writing a postcard
          4. Writing a letter

Teen 5   1. Writing an informal letter
          2. Answering a questionnaire
          3. Writing a formal letter
          4. Introducing yourself

Teen 6   1. Describing an object
          2. Describing people
          3. Sequencing in writing (timeline)
          4. Writing a narrative

Teen 7   1. Freewriting, writing a journal
          2. Description
          3. Comparison and contrast

Teen 8   1. Description
          2. Narrative

Teen 9   1. Argumentation
          2. Narrative

Luciane agreed with this plan, and we brainstormed ideas for putting it into practice. We wanted our students to be both creative and critical. We wanted them to be able to write, understand their mistakes, and correct their own errors. These ideas fit in with the view of writing as a process rather than as a product (Raimes 1983). Alumni was already working with the writing process in other courses. I had had the chance to work with it when I was a primary school teacher and so had firsthand experience of its effectiveness. We thus decided to adopt the writing process in our teen supplement.

The writing process gives the students the opportunity to improve their writing through systematic self-correction: After a topic is brainstormed during some kind of preliminary work done in the group, the writer writes a first draft. Then the students exchange their drafts and, with the aid of a checklist and a list of symbols for error correction (see Appendix B), they give feedback on their friends' writing. After that, the writers read their peers' comments and make the necessary changes: This is called the second draft. Then the teacher reads the students' drafts and gives feedback in the form of written comments. The last step of this process requires the students to rewrite their drafts again, producing a third draft. This way the process is emphasized, not the product.

However, for this writing process to be feasible and successful, I would have to motivate the students to write. Creating the desire to write about something would necessitate a series of steps leading up to the writing activity. This preparation stage, which I called *prework,* was crucial for the development of the process. This stage would provide the students with the feeling that whenever they were supposed to sit down and write, they would already have in mind all the ideas and vocabulary they needed. This stage would have to include an activity that was dynamic and challenging and that brought in new vocabulary as well as helped them develop new ideas about a certain topic.

Another factor that I thought quite important for the engagement of my students in the writing process was interaction or collaboration. In this regard, I was influenced by a university course I was taking in which interaction was seen as extremely significant in any learning process. Many linguists and psychologists agree that interaction is crucial as a means of exchanging knowledge that would engender both development and learning. Vygotsky (1988) points out that there is no development or learning without interaction among people and that the human being first experiences active problem-solving activities in the presence of others. Rivers (1987) says that communication derives essentially from interaction in which someone has something to share with someone else, who is interested and active while the interest lasts. Allwright (1984) believes that exchange is the basic unit of discourse. Linguistic interaction is a collaborative activity involving the establishment of a triangular relationship among the sender, the receiver, and the context of the situation. Davis (1989) perhaps best summarizes the importance of interaction within the classroom: Interaction is the process in which each student is in charge of building knowledge, so that the solution is reached through a common effort of cooperation and mutual help. Having all these ideas in mind, I wanted the students to cooperate and interact during the prework so that they could together learn how to be better writers. They would be learning about each other's experiences, which would help them be more creative and organize their ideas more easily.

Because I was most concerned about the process, I spent a long time working on developing the prework activities, where students would be interacting and learning at the same time. The actual writing task would then be just a matter of organizing ideas previously discussed. During this prework stage, students would already be thinking of what to write about without even realizing that they were doing so. I felt that if the prework activities were done well, the actual writing would be easier. (Examples of prework activities for students in Teen 6 appear in Appendix C.)

It took us about twenty days to develop the activities for level 4. Then, while Teen 4 students were in class working with the activities, I started writing level 5 activities. Thus when the Teen 4 students started level 5, they would already have had one semester of the new supplement.

As soon as the material for level 5 was ready, I planned a workshop for all the teen teachers. The importance and objectives of the writing process and the prework were discussed. I wanted the teachers to understand what I meant by "writing process" – that meaning and content are of primary importance for the writer. In a process approach, the process is not linear at all; it is cyclical, and the writers move back and forth on a continuum, discovering, analyzing, and synthesizing ideas. The teachers should have a clear understanding of the importance of the process in contrast to the product.

I conducted the workshop in a very practical way. First, I had the teachers work with the definitions of process and product, and for this purpose I had characteristics of both written on cards, which they had to separate according to the two definitions. After that, they had to match the three stages of the writing process with activities that should be done in each one. They summarized the information as follows: The first stage of the activities would consist of prewriting (prework). In this stage, students would be discovering new ideas, exchanging knowledge, gathering information, thinking of what to write about, and asking for new vocabulary and expressions to voice their feelings and thoughts. This stage is the planning stage of writing. The second stage is the actual writing. For the first draft, they would just jot down ideas, but as they go to the second and third drafts, they would synthesize, organize, and clarify the writing. The last stage is revision, which would be considered part of the writing stage. It is at this stage that the students analyze their writing. Through the process of revising and editing, the writers refine their thoughts, structures, and grammar over successive drafts.

Another aspect emphasized in the workshop was the definition of a good writer and how we teachers can help our students become competent writers. A lot was said about the contrast between an unskilled writer and an experienced one. The teachers had to analyze statements about the two types of writers and identify which referred to experienced writers ("They consult their background knowledge"; "They let their ideas incubate"; "They don't worry about format and grammar at first"). We concluded that we wanted our students to behave as experienced writers and learn to plan and to request and use feedback to rewrite and revise their writing.

After discussing the theory, the second step was to have the teachers do one complete activity, as if they were Teen 4 students. The teachers showed a lot of interest and were very curious to see how students would react to the new supplement.

Evaluation of activities was also discussed. It was suggested that teachers should be much more concerned with the students' attitudes than with the students' mistakes. Teachers should ask questions such as these: Did the students actively participate? Did they put an effort into doing the writing? Did they hand in all the assignments? Did the teacher always give positive feedback? We wanted to grade not our students' writing but rather their attitude toward writing. The questions that Luciane and I had formulated would help teachers observe students and grade them. We believed that if we had students motivated to write, there was no need for formal grading. We thought that telling them about their progress would be enough for them to try harder on the next activity.

As I piloted the writing folder (the name we gave to the writing supplement; see Appendix A) for levels 8 and 9, I tested the new material with these classes. Very few changes were made, but I felt that these were special groups and I was too excited to be able to be more critical about the material. During the next year, when the writing supplement was in use in levels 4 and 5, I regularly asked teachers how they were doing with it. At the end of the year, I had a meeting with the level 4 and 5 teachers at which I raised the subject of writing. The teachers' feedback was categorized into positive and negative aspects.

Positive aspects: Students were not complaining about having to write.
Students never said, "I don't know what to write about."

	Students had fun commenting on their peers' work. Students had better results on the quizzes given during the semester.
Negative aspects:	Teachers were short of time and couldn't manage to do all the prework and peer-feedback in class. Students frequently didn't do their homework (drafts), which interrupted the process of giving feedback.

Based on this feedback, I decided that the first negative aspect could be addressed by reducing the number of activities from four to three. To address the second negative aspect, a grade for "written work" was added to the students' report cards, for we know that teens work better when they are being graded formally. We felt that the grade would ensure that they do their homework.

At the end of every semester, we give our students a course evaluation questionnaire. When the writing activities were being taught at all levels, we included a question related to the writing activities. It asks the students whether they consider the writing activities to be "excellent," "good," "regular," or "weak." Based on the responses to the first semester's questionnaire, it seems that there is a positive attitude toward the writing activities: 38 percent of our students rated them "excellent" or "good," and only 13 percent considered them "regular" or "weak." The second semester's questionnaire showed even better results: 45 percent "excellent" or "good," 13 percent "regular" or "weak."

The experience of designing a course meant a lot to me. Being creative, helping my students be better writers in English, and working with teachers so that more students learn was very rewarding. Besides, it is always a victory to face a challenging battle and win. Nowadays, designing a course is not a battle anymore, but a task that helps me grow as a teacher and as a person. I know that I can do it, as any teacher can.

Appendix A: Introduction to writing supplement

Associação Alumni
Department of English
Teen 6   Teacher's Sheet

Writing Folder

Introduction

Teaching writing involves careful planning as well as clear knowledge of the whole writing process developed from Teen 4 on. Not only objectives have to be established but also the steps to be followed. The activities in the student's folder will help students organize their ideas clearly and coherently so that they arrive at a correct and interesting final product.

Folder

The writing folder presents three or four different activities to be done in class or at home. Many of the instructions given suggest that your students work in pairs or with a group. You can use checklists in the folder to help you.

1. List of symbols for error correction
2. Checklist for feedback

Activities and materials

Activity	Type	Materials
1	Describing an object	"Describing an Object" transparency
2	Describing people	Matching cards "Describing People" transparency
3	Sequence in writing	Sentences on strips 3 transparencies, A, B_1, and B_2
4	Writing a narrative	—

Procedures

Lead-in activities: For each of the writing activities, there are a
                             number of lead-in activities that should be
                             done in class under your guidance. It is ex-

tremely important that your students feel motivated when doing the activities, for they are not only the warm-up but also the key for writing successfully. Clear directions are given on the student's sheet.

Writing a first draft: Students are supposed to jot down their ideas. No set form should be expected at this time. At this stage, they should be working on ideas and how to organize them and not on structures or forms. It is not teacher-corrected, and it is followed by peer feedback (students use the peer feedback sheet to share what they have written in pairs).

Writing a second draft: This activity is based on the first draft. It can be done in class or at home. Students are supposed to pay attention to both content and form. Students can use the checklist for revision. It is followed by teacher feedback.

Please observe the following:
— Be very objective.
— Pay attention to forms and structures, but always give positive feedback.
— Circle mistakes so that students can discover why something is wrong.
— Cross out repetitive words and substitute synonyms.
— Use checklists while revising and the list of symbols for error correction to help you.

Writing a third draft: This activity can also be done in class or at home. It should be done based on the first and second drafts and their correction. The checklists can still be useful. When grading the writing activities, the teacher should be much more concerned with students' attitudes rather than with students' mistakes. Did your students actively participate? Did you feel they put an effort into the activity? Did they hand in all their assignments? Do not forget to give students positive feedback.

Appendix B: Symbols for Error Correction and Checklist for Peer Feedback

Associação Alumni
Department of English
Teens 4, 5, and 6

Symbols for Error Correction

Symbol	Meaning	Example
SP	spelling error	She's a stu^{SP}dant.
\WM/	word missing	They\WM/born in São Paulo.
/	omit this word	They are ⱥ good friends.
WW	wrong word	I live at^{WW} São Paulo.
P, ⱷ	punctuation errors	They both, speak French^P
⌐*WO*⌐	word order errors	I went yesterday to the club.
C, ¢	capitalization error	^Cboth students like ¢Languages.
VT	verb tense	I go^{VT} to Guarujá last weekend.
⌣	connect to make one word	I forgot to do the home⌣work.
/	separate the words	This book is science/fiction.

Checklist for peer feedback

1. Content
   a. Is the writing interesting? How do you know it is interesting?
   b. Which part do you like best? Why? Underline the best sentence.
   c. Would you add or suggest more details to make the situation, description, or narrative clearer?
2. Organization
   a. Can you summarize the main idea?
   b. Is the writing organized? Is there anything that you don't understand?
   c. Would you change the order of any sentence?
   d. Are the events told in the order that they happened? Were transition words used? Which ones?
3. Editing
   a. Did you notice any spelling or punctuation mistakes? If so, use the list of symbols for error correction.
   b. Did you notice any grammar errors: in subject-verb agreement, tense of verbs, word order, and so on?
   c. Is the vocabulary varied? If not, suggest synonyms.

Appendix C: Activities

Associação Alumni
Department of English
Teen 6   Student's Sheet

Activity 1: Describing an Object

Part A – Looking for specific vocabulary

Directions 1: Find 15 words in the grid below. They can be used to
describe objects. You can only read words across or down.
Work in pairs.

O	V	A	L	P	P	O	M	L	P
A	B	R	I	G	H	T	U	W	L
B	O	C	G	D	C	O	C	O	A
F	T	G	H	H	I	P	H	O	S
J	T	S	T	R	I	P	E	D	T
K	O	L	L	O	N	G	A	E	I
M	M	N	N	U	O	P	P	N	C
G	R	E	E	N	Q	R	X	Z	S
T	U	V	W	D	Z	C	U	T	E
X	Z	X	A	F	L	U	F	F	Y

Now write the words here: _____

Directions 2: Look at the object you brought, and write words that come
into your mind when you look at it and feel it. Your teacher
can help you with additional vocabulary.

_____

_____

Directions 3: With a partner, write sentences using the words you have
written about the object.

_____

_____

Part B – Describing an object

Directions 1: Look at the transparency, and talk about your own object
using the words and sentences you have written in Part A.
You may take notes if you wish.

Directions 2: Write a first draft

(*Use the space below to describe your object. Do not forget to use
all the information in the previous exercises.*)

Directions 3: Peer feedback

(*This space should be used for peer feedback.*)

Directions 4: Writing a second draft

(*Use your friend's feedback to rewrite your description.*)

Directions 5: Teacher's feedback

(*This space should be used for your teacher's comments.*)

Directions 6: Writing a third draft

(*Use this space to revise your work after your teacher has given
you feedback.*)

Associação Alumni
Department of English
Teen 6   Teacher's Sheet

Activity 1: Describing an Object

(*Note:* It is essential that students bring any object they like to class.)

Part A – Looking for specific vocabulary

Directions 1: Students should look for specific vocabulary, in pairs.

Answer key

O	V	A	L	P	P	O	M	L	P
A	B	R	I	G	H	T	U	W	L
B	O	C	G	D	C	O	C	O	A
F	T	G	H	H	I	P	H	O	S
J	T	S	T	R	I	P	E	D	T
K	O	L	L	O	N	G	A	E	I
M	M	N	N	U	O	P	P	N	C
G	R	E	E	N	Q	R	X	Z	S
T	U	V	W	D	Z	C	U	T	E
X	Z	X	A	F	L	U	F	F	Y

Directions 2: Be ready to help your students with additional vocabulary.

Directions 3: Students work in pairs.

Part B – Describing an object

Directions 1 to 6: See student's sheet.

Teen 6 – Writing activity 1   Teacher's materials

Describing an Object – Transparency

1. How
   When   get this object?
   Where
2. What/look like?
3. What/feel/when/touch it?
4. What memories/it/bring you?
5. Why/object/important to you?

Associação Alumni
Department of English
Teen 6   Student's Sheet

Activity 2: Describing People

Part A – Matching cards: questions and answers

Directions: Frank asks some questions about Annie's sister. Read the cards
and match the questions with their answers.
Check with your teacher.
Now copy the questions from the cards and write what you
would answer about yourself.

QUESTIONS   *ANSWERS*

_____

_____
_____
_____
_____
_____

Part B – Descriptive paragraph on transparency

Directions: Read the transparency silently, analyze it with a friend and try
to decide what the main ideas for the following sentences are.

Sentence 1: _____

Sentences 2 and 3: _____

Sentences 4 and 5: _____

Sentence 6: _____

Part C – Writing a descriptive paragraph

Directions 1: Writing a first draft

(Think of a person you know well, and write a paragraph about her
or him. Parts A and B will help you develop your work, so do not
forget to go back to them whenever necessary.)

_____.

_____

Directions 2: Peer feedback

(This space should be used for peer feedback.)

Directions 3: Writing a second draft

(Use your friend's feedback to rewrite your description.)

Directions 4: Teacher's feedback

(This space should be used for your teacher's comments.)

Directions 5: Writing a third draft

(Use this space to revise your work after your teacher has given you feedback.)

Associação Alumni
Department of English
Teen 6   Teacher's Sheet

Activity 2: Describing People

Part A – Matching cards: questions and answers

Directions: Students should match the cards (questions and answers). Help them differentiate be like X, look like X, and the other questions.

Part B – Descriptive paragraph on transparency

Directions: Analyze the paragraph with your students and help them elicit the following ideas.

Sentence 1:   Gives a general impression of Jack
Sentences 2 and 3: Say what he looks like (appearance)
Sentences 4 and 5: Say what he is like (personality)
Sentence 6:   Says why people like Jack (conclusion)

Part C – Writing a descriptive paragraph

Directions 1 to 5: See student's sheet.

Describing People – Matching cards

What does she dislike?
What is she like?
What does she look like?
What does she like?
How is she these days?
Who does she look like?

She hates having to wake up early and gets bored watching TV.
Her loose, wavy hair hangs down to the back of her waist. She has bangs
    over her forehead that almost hide her pale blue eyes. She isn't very tall
    or slim.
She's a little shy, but she's fun to be with. She has the irritating habit of
    biting her nails. Apart from that, she's always friendly and positive, once
    you know her well.
Baseball, Italian food, video games, and classical music.
We don't look much alike. In general, she resembles my father's side of the
    family, but she has my mother's eyes.
She looks exhausted now. She's really busy at work and needs a vacation.

Describing People – Transparency

My cousin, Jack Stone, is a very popular fellow in the neighborhood.
He's plain-looking and of medium height. His dark eyes are friendly, and he
is always smiling under his dark moustache. Jack is a helpful person: He is
always ready to give a neighbor a lift or to fix the boys' motorbikes. He is
outgoing and loves to go camping with his friends. Everybody likes Jack
because he's such a simple, easygoing, and uncomplicated person.

Associação Alumni
Department of English
Teen 6   Student's Sheet

Activity 3: Sequence in Writing

Part A – Working with transition words and expressions

Directions 1: Put the sentences on the strips in chronological order; then
check your answers against transparency A. Circle the transition expressions, and write them in the space below.

Directions 2: Read the text on transparency B1, and insert a transition
word or expression in each blank. Check your answers
against transparency B2, and write down the transition
words.

Directions 3: When are transition words or expressions used? In pairs,
write your conclusions in the space below.

Would you include other transition words?

Part B – Working with a time line

Directions 1: Have you ever seen or done a time line? Look at Santos
Dumont's time line, and read it to your friend as if it were a
paragraph. Begin like this: When Santos Dumont was a
teenager he showed . . .

Santos Dumont's Time Line

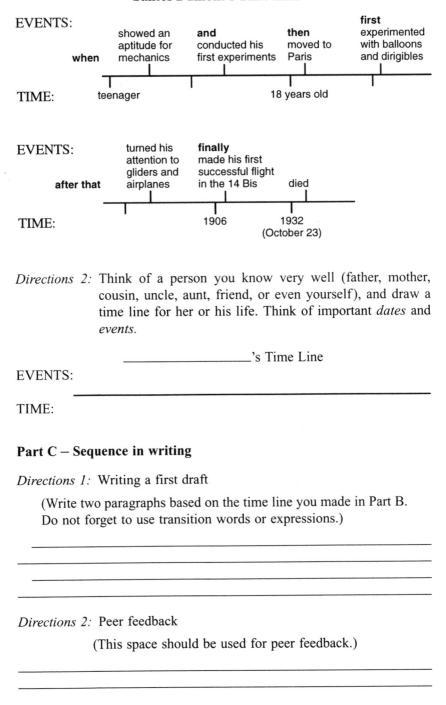

EVENTS:

	showed an aptitude for	**and** conducted his	**then** moved to	**first** experimented with balloons
when	mechanics	first experiments	Paris	and dirigibles

TIME: teenager   18 years old

EVENTS:

	turned his attention to gliders and	**finally** made his first successful flight	
after that	airplanes	in the 14 Bis	died

TIME: 1906   1932
                                            (October 23)

Directions 2: Think of a person you know very well (father, mother, cousin, uncle, aunt, friend, or even yourself), and draw a time line for her or his life. Think of important *dates* and *events*.

_____'s Time Line

EVENTS:

_____

TIME:

Part C – Sequence in writing

Directions 1: Writing a first draft

(Write two paragraphs based on the time line you made in Part B. Do not forget to use transition words or expressions.)

_____
_____
_____
_____

Directions 2: Peer feedback

(This space should be used for peer feedback.)

_____
_____

Directions 3: Writing a second draft.

(Use your friend's feedback as a guide to rewrite your first draft.)

_____

_____

_____

_____

Directions 4: Teacher's feedback

(This space should be used for your teacher's comments.)

_____

_____

_____

_____

Directions 5: Writing a third draft

(Use this space to revise your work after your teacher has given you feedback.)

_____

_____

_____

_____

Activity 3: Sequence in Writing

Part A – Working with transition words and expressions

Directions 1: Hand out strips to students, and have them put the sentences in chronological order. Then project transparency A for the students to check sentence order. The students should circle the transition words: *then, therefore, after that, first, then,* and *finally.*

Directions 2: Students should insert a transition word or expression in each blank of transparency B1. Transparency B2 will help with correction.

Directions 3: Help your students answer the questions.

Part B – Working with a time line

Directions 1: Students work in pairs. You can give more examples if necessary.

Directions 2: Monitor your students.

Part C – Sequence in writing

Directions 1 to 5: See student's sheet.

Sentences on strips

After graduating, she decided to get a job.

Therefore, she moved near the university and lived with some friends.

The university was far from her home, and she could not drive there every day.

First, she worked as a receptionist, but she did not like the hours.

Then she got a job as a secretary, but she did not like typing and filing.

Then her father and mother moved to Los Angeles, and Trudy went to a large university.

Finally, Trudy moved to San Francisco, where she is now teaching handicapped children, a job she really enjoys.

Trudy was born in a small town in California.

She lived there until the age of 17.

Transparency A

Trudy was born in a small town in California. She lived there until the age of 17. Then her father and mother moved to Los Angeles, and Trudy went to a large university. The university was far from her home, and she could not drive there every day. Therefore, she moved near the university and lived with some friends.

After graduating, she decided to get a job. First, she worked as a receptionist, but she did not like the hours. Then she got a job as a secretary, but she did not like typing and filing. Finally, Trudy moved to San Francisco, where she is now teaching handicapped children, a job she really enjoys.

Transparency B1

How to drive a car

_____ open the car door, get in to the car, and sit in the driver's seat.

_____ fasten the safety belt; _____ you might get a fine or hurt yourself badly if there is a accident. _____ make sure that the gear lever is in the neutral position. Insert the key in the ignition, and turn it to start the engine. _____ you can drive away immediately, it is a good idea to let the engine warm up a little first.

_____ step on the clutch and put the car into first gear.

_____, release the clutch, step on the gas pedal, and . . . have a nice drive!

Transparency B2

How to drive a car

⟨FIRST⟩ open the car door, get in to the car, and sit in the driver's seat.

⟨NEXT⟩ fasten the safety belt; ⟨OTHERWISE⟩ you might get a fine or hurt yourself badly if there is a accident. ⟨THEN⟩ make sure that the gear lever is in the neutral position. Insert the key in the ignition, and turn it to start the engine. ⟨ALTHOUGH⟩ you can drive away immediately, it is a good idea to let the engine warm up a little first. ⟨THEN⟩ step on the clutch and put the car into first gear. ⟨FINALLY⟩, release the clutch, step on the gas pedal and . . . have a nice drive!

Associação Alumni
Department of English
Teen 6   Student's Sheet

Activity 4: Writing a Narrative

Part A – Reading an anecdote

Directions 1: Read the text in the box. Then, in pairs, answer the questions
below it.

> One day Rodney Monroe, a teacher in a school, asked one of his pupils,
> Mary Smith, to go to the blackboard and write out an exercise. When Mary
> reached the front of the room, her fellow classmates began to laugh. Mary
> usually did something funny whenever she got the chance, so Rodney was
> usually on guard for her pranks. But this time he really could not at first
> understand why the class was laughing at her. Then he noticed her stock-
> ings. She was wearing one red stocking, but the other one was blue.
>
> "What unusual stockings, Mary," Rodney remarked, hoping he could
> prevent further laughter from the class.
>
> "I am so glad you like them," Mary replied with a serious face. "I have
> another pair at home just like this one."
>
> He noticed that this remark delighted the class even more. Rodney has
> decided that he should not call on Mary again for some time.

(From Dean 1988)

1. Is the writer only an observer of the action, or does he participate in it?

   _____

   _____

2. Suppose you are Rodney. Make the changes necessary for your first-
   person point of view.

   _____

   _____

3. Observe the underlined words. Try to read the passage without them.
   Can you do it? Why are they so important?

   _____

   _____

4. When writing a narrative, we relate a series of events. This means that
   we tell what happened in chronological order or time sequence, and
   _____ are essential to serve as bridges between spaces
   of time. The use of _____ is another way to indicate
   sequence. You must also decide if you will be an active participant
   (_____ person) or an observer of the action
   (_____ person).

Part B – Interviewing people

Directions 1:   Work in small groups. Think of an anecdote that you have told about yourself or about someone you know. Jot down some notes about it.

Directions 2:   Now interview one of your friends about his or her anecdote, and take notes in the space below.

Part C – Writing an anecdote

Directions 1:   Writing a first draft

(Use one of the following phrases to introduce your own anecdote or someone else's.)

Something rather odd happened last week.
We had a strange experience while on vacation last year.
You'll never guess what   <u>(*name*)</u>   did.

Directions 2:   Peer feedback

(This space should be used for peer feedback.)

Directions 3:   Writing a second draft

(Use your friend's feedback to rewrite your narrative.)

Directions 4:   Teacher's feedback

(This space should be used for your teacher's comments.)

Directions 5:   Writing a third draft

(Use this space to rewrite your work after your teacher has given you feedback.)

Associação Alumni
Department of English
Teen 6   Teacher's Sheet

Activity 4: Writing a Narrative

Part A – Reading an anecdote

Directions: Students read the text and answer the questions in pairs. Emphasize the use of transition words, verb tenses, and the writer's participation or not when telling a story.

Part B – Interviewing people

Directions: Make clear to the students the meaning of an anecdote (a short, interesting, amusing true story). Students should take notes of the transition words used and the events in the chronological order in which they happened.

Part C – Writing an anecdote

Directions 1 to 5: See student's sheet.

ANALYSIS AND TASKS

A variety of reasons – some internal to the institution, some external, and some pedagogical – led to the creation of the writing supplement described here. The teen students were tested on their writing abilities but were not taught writing and so fared poorly on the tests. Those who continued with courses at a higher level, which emphasized reading and writing, were not prepared. Writing was seen as a way to reinforce other skills, as well as a skill that could be useful outside of the classroom context. Thus M. Estela Pinheiro Franco and her colleague, Luciane Nunes, had a solid rationale for proposing the writing supplement. One of the constraints they recognized in making their proposal was that it should cause a minimum of disruption to the curriculum already in place.

Students' needs per se were not an issue, which is often the case in an EFL context. Although she could assume that the students might write in English outside of class, meeting the demands of those out-of-class situations was not an overriding concern. Once given approval, Pinheiro saw the main challenge as figuring out how to get her students to be engaged in the activities, how to motivate them. Hence a lot of her energy was spent looking at who the students were, what kinds of activities engaged them in other classes, what challenged and interested them. This reflection and assessment process led her to think about the kinds of materials and themes on which she could build her syllabus.

From Pinheiro's narrative, we can see that for her, developing materials is synonymous with developing activities. For example, the time line described in Activity 3 (Appendix C) is both a material that is handed out to the students and an activity that they are to do something with. She designed four activities for each level. In Pinheiro's syllabus, an "activity" was actually a set of tasks that culminated in the students writing something, such as a narrative. It was important that the material be interesting to students and that each task introduce something new so that students would feel challenged. How the students worked with one another was also unimportant factor. Theories of how writing is learned, as well as theories of learning played an important role in how the students were asked to work with each other in carrying out the activities. Specifically, Pinheiro's experience with the process approach to writing – teaching writing as a process rather than as a means to a prescribed end or product, led her to build in peer review and critique. Theories about the role of interaction in learning led her to design activities that required collaboration on the part of the students. Pinheiro wanted her students to be both creative and critical, so it was not just a matter of their enjoying their work and being motivated but also of their learning and making progress. An emphasis on writing as a process facilitated this. In addition, it was important that students want to write, not be afraid or discouraged; consequently, the tasks consisted of a series of steps whose natural outcome was a piece of written work.

Sequencing the activities, both within each level and across levels was an important issue to be tackled. Pinheiro looked at sequencing in four ways: (1) in terms of the complexity of the type of writing, narration being considered less complex than argumentation, for example; (2) in terms of the amount of writing required (less at beginning levels, more at higher levels); (3) in terms of the relative concreteness and structure of the tasks, with more concrete, structured tasks preceding tasks that required more student input, imagination, and initiative; and (4) in terms of how one task built on the preceding one, so that by the time students got to the final writing task, they were thoroughly prepared – as Pinheiro put it, the students would have "the feeling that whenever they were supposed to sit down and write, they would already have in mind all the ideas and vocabulary they needed." She called the steps leading up to the writing "prework."

Pinheiro was also responsible for training other teachers in the use of her syllabus. She had two important objectives in conducting her training: to ensure that teachers had a clear understanding of the theory underlying her syllabus and how it was manifested in the activities and to motivate them to want to teach the supplement. She followed many of the same principles in her training session as she did in her syllabus design: seeking ways to engage the teachers, planning the activities so that each one prepared the participants for the next, and asking them to collaborate, culminating in experiencing one of the activities as a learner.

Evaluation of the supplement, which came from formal and informal input from the teachers and from student questionnaires, prompted certain modifications. Pinheiro points out that it was difficult for her to evaluate the effectiveness of the materials when she herself was teaching with them because she was so invested in their success. A crucial aspect of the success of the writing supplement was the time and support Pinheiro was given by her institution to design and pilot the activities.

FOCUS ON SELECTING AND DEVELOPING MATERIALS AND ACTIVITIES

1. In designing the materials and activities, Pinheiro's central question was how to motivate students. To answer this question, she considered who her students were, their interests, their attitudes toward the subject, and the types of activities that engaged them in class.

   Answer the following questions in relation to your students. If you do not know the answers, consider ways you could find out the answers. Add questions you feel are pertinent.

- Who are my students?
- What are their interests?
- What are their attitudes toward the subject matter? Towards being a student?
- What are the types of activities which engage them and why?

2. Pinheiro had several criteria in designing the activities in her writing supplement: (a) that the topics be of interest to the students; (b) that they feel each activity had a purpose; (c) that the activities challenge students and teach them something new, and (d) that their success depend on students working together and exchanging ideas. Which criteria are relevant to your course? Which criteria would you add? Describe how an activity or set of activities from your course fulfills your criteria.

3. As described in the analysis, Pinheiro considered several factors in organizing and sequencing her material.

   Consult the activities for Teen 6 in Appendix C. Find an example for each of these criteria.

   - More highly structured activities prepare students for less structured ones in which they take more initiative.
   - Material that requires relatively less complex thinking or skills precedes material that requires relatively more complex thinking or skills.
   - Each task or activity prepares students for the next one, or, conversely, each task builds on the previous one.
   - Similar themes (in Pinheiro's case, written discourse types) are revisited throughout the course, with more complex and demanding treatment each time.
   - Each activity is broken down into lead-in tasks, which prepare students for the culminating task, in this case, the particular type of composition.

4. Which of the criteria listed in question 3 are useful for you to consider in sequencing the content and material in your course? Why? Describe or prepare an example from your course that exemplifies each criterion you have chosen.

References

Allwright, R. 1984. Why don't learners learn what teachers teach? In *The Interaction Hypothesis*. Lancaster, England: University of Lancaster.

Davis, C. et al. *Papel e Valor das Interações Sociais na Sala de Aula* [The Role and Value of Social Interaction in the Classroom]. Caderno de Pesquisa, #71, 49–54, November 1989.

Dean, M. 1988. *Write It: Writing Skills for Intermediate Learners of English.* Cambridge: Cambridge University Press.

Raimes, A. 1983. *Techniques in Teaching Writing.* New York: Oxford University Press.

Rivers, W. 1987. *Interactive Language Teaching.* New York: Cambridge University Press.

Vygotsky, L. S. 1988. *A Formação Social da Mente* [Mind in Society]. São Paulo: Martins Fontes.

7 Planning an advanced listening comprehension elective for Japanese college students

Barbara Fujiwara

Barbara Fujiwara's interest in the learning strategies of "good learners" led to the research for her master's thesis, which in turn led her to agree to develop this new course at the junior college where she teaches. A teacher and teacher educator who lives and teaches in Japan, Fujiwara began her career there teaching English to middle and high school students. She has recently developed seminar courses on intercultural communication and on women's issues. In this chapter, Fujiwara provides the reader with a window into the way one teacher makes sense of theory in her classroom practice and transforms both in the process. She has written about her experience in the form of letters to a colleague.

The course development focuses for this chapter are selecting and developing materials and activities, and organization of content and activities. Consider the following questions as you read:

Why is the selection of material a critical consideration for Fujiwara?
What systems does she set in motion to organize the course, and what role do the students play in carrying out the systems?

April 14

I have been asked to write a chapter about the listening elective I'm going to teach this term. I must admit that the thought of having to describe my inchoate, confused, and intuitive method of course design seems somewhat daunting. I can already see myself trying to organize the messiness of my thought processes into categories, models, patterns. I am reminded of a key moment in my internship for my M.A. in teaching when my supervisor asked me as we were going over a lesson plan, "Why are you doing that activity?" I felt a bolt of anxiety in my stomach. "Why? Yes, why, indeed?"

Though now I do try to articulate objectives, my method of planning still begins with activities and visions of the class. It's only when I look at the visions that I can begin to analyze why I'm doing what I'm doing. I also need to be in dialogue with students, so it's hard for me to design a year's course in the abstract. Just as my language-learning process is no longer in awareness, so my planning process is based on layers and layers of assumptions, experiences, and knowledge. I have to dig down deep to find out why I make the decisions I do.

So it won't be easy for me to describe my planning process, but the timing is right, as I am just about to begin a new course for our junior college. Last October, I was asked to teach advanced listening, a new elective course for second-year students to begin in April, just a few days from now. We have a required first-year listening comprehension course, called language lab, which is taught by a well-organized and well-coordinated group of Japanese teachers. Student feedback indicated that some students were interested in continuing their listening study so we decided to add advanced listening to the curriculum.

It was expected that one of the language lab (LL) teachers would teach the course, but their schedules were full, so I was asked to teach it, probably because of my master's thesis research on learner training in listening strategies (Fujiwara 1990). I was somewhat taken aback because my research had been on the development of a listening diary homework program and I hadn't actually done much in-class work on listening comprehension since coming to the college although I had done a lot of beginning listening when I was teaching at the junior and senior high school level some years ago. In addition, I felt uncomfortable about teaching in the language lab, partly because our state-of-the-art equipment seemed terrifyingly complex and partly because I prefer a more interactive teaching style than seemed possible in a language lab. I had observed a few LL classes and was extremely impressed, but it was hard to imagine myself up at the console, efficiently directing the students to put this set of tapes in and that set out.

However, no one else had an interest in listening comprehension, so I accepted, and with only a few weeks to think about the new course, I had to write a course description. I was quite busy at the time, so I tried to write something that would be vague enough for me to do what I wanted to do after I had more time to think about it yet clear enough so that students could decide if they were interested in the course. Some important considerations were evident immediately.

The first consideration was helping students become independent listening learners. I believe that independent study is particularly important at the college level to make up for the limited contact hours and to prepare students for self-instruction after graduation. A college course in Japan typically has only 40 contact hours over a year, that is, 26 class meetings of 90 minutes each. Because my junior college students have only two years at the college, I have increasingly emphasized learner training in my second-year courses. I had developed the listening diary homework program for my oral English students, but I wanted to incorporate learner training in advanced listening as well. My aim is for students to leave the course with an interest in and ideas for using the abundance of English-language listening materials available in Japan, as I believe self-instruction in listening will be an important way to maintain and improve their language skills.

The second consideration was providing a rich and deep context for language learning. I have been interested in this idea for a number of reasons. One inspiration was a lecture by Liz Heron I attended during graduate school in which she described a content-based remedial reading course for both native speakers and ESL students that she had developed. All the readings were on one topic, evolution, although they varied in difficulty and genre, thus providing for both individualization and a common discussion topic. She believed that having the readings on the same topic enabled students to progress through Chall's five stages of reading development (Chall 1983).

My own experience in teaching my second-year seminar on cross-cultural communication has convinced me of the efficacy of a content-based curriculum in teaching language skills as well. I had actually been thinking about changing my seminar topic to "contemporary lifestyles and issues in the United Kingdom and the United States" but upon being asked to teach the new course, I decided to use this topic as the context for advanced listening instead. We have had a lot of faculty room discussion about whether and how to make the Oral English II course different from Oral English I, and some teachers have decided to add more content in the second year. I thought that having a content-based curriculum would make the course different from the first-year language lab course.

A third consideration was keeping students in the course. The course is an elective, which means that students can drop it with no effect on graduation. A friend who teaches an elective at our four-year college has told me how discouraging it is to see the numbers drop week after week. I definitely did not want that to happen because it might mean that the course would get dropped from the curriculum. Therefore, I wanted to have a lot of student choice about materials and process, as I think that leads to higher student involvement. I also decided it would be important to state that there would be homework in the course description to ensure that I would attract motivated students who were willing to work.

With the three considerations in mind, I wrote the course description as follows:

In this course, students will increase and improve their listening strategies and skills. A variety of audio and video materials focusing on contemporary lifestyles and issues in the United States and the United Kingdom will be used in class. Students will also be expected to do extensive listening practice outside of class, including designing and carrying out their own listening projects.

In November, preregistration was held, and seventy-eight students signed up for the course, which was limited to forty. To select the forty, I had the students write essays on the topic "what and how I want to study in advanced listening," and only thirty-eight students wrote the essays, so I accepted them all. The overenrollment of the course gave me an unusual opportunity to have some student input in course planning.

The next deadline I had to face was the middle of December, when we placed textbook orders. I had two main options to consider. One was to go completely with a course of my own making in which I would gather materials from movies, TV, and other sources. I felt reluctant to do this because of the huge time investment it would require, getting the videos from abroad, viewing and selecting them, editing, and so on. At that time, I didn't even have a VCR, although in January I finally bought one, justifying it as something I needed for my work.

So I decided to go with the second option and use published works as the main course materials and try to collect other materials for supplementary use. Colleagues stressed the need for variety in a language lab course, so I thought it would be best to use both video and audio, but I wanted materials that would fit in with the course content. A friend, Sherraid Scott, who had used several video courses, suggested *The Secret Diary of Adrian Mole, Aged 13¾,* a British TV program that a Japanese publisher was selling as a video and text. She thought the text was too easy but highly recommended the video. I had seen a few episodes at her house the year before and felt that the video had appropriate content (family problems, etc).

It was more problematic choosing an audio course because I wanted one that would combine strategy training and content. Most of the listening texts had one disadvantage or another. Some emphasized task listening, which the students were already doing in the first-year LL course and which had little cultural content. Some were too conversational, duplicating the work done in oral English, and others emphasized academic listening skills and included scientific and other inappropriate content. Finally, I found myself torn between two choices, both of which seemed difficult but perhaps all right for "advanced" listening. One was a BBC course, *How to Listen* (Geddes 1988), which consisted of listening extracts from BBC radio broadcasts and offered the best training program in listening strategies I had seen in a text. For the most part, the topics of the listening extracts could loosely fit under the rubric "contemporary lifestyles and issues," although a few, like the extract on camels, could not by any stretch of the imagination. The other, *Talk Radio* (Sadow and Sather 1987), a collection of actual conversations from an American radio talk show, had great topics but a rather small variety of listening exercises. Though primarily a listening skills course, it also had material for other skills that I didn't need or want. Not being able to decide between the two courses, I decided to choose both, as together they would provide a good combination of skills training and cultural learning.

Once the text decision was made, I put the course out of my mind except for worrying about collecting supplementary materials. The phrase "variety of materials" haunted me, as it had been picked up by the students in their essays, in which they had said how they were looking forward to studying songs, movies, animated cartoons, news programs, TV programs, and so on. In terms of their awareness of possible materials, they were definitely advanced. I began to harass my family in the United States and friends in the United Kingdom to "send videos," and I would frantically watch various broadcast satellite TV programs, asking myself, "Should I tape this? Would the students understand this? Does this show some aspect of contemporary life?" Then, suddenly, I got the idea – partly from one student essay in which a student had said she wanted students to choose the listening materials and partly from two colleagues who had their students do group projects on songs in Oral English II – of having the students do group projects in which they would select listening materials and teach them to the other students. What a brilliant idea! I immediately stopped my frantic search.

In March, during spring vacation, I began to think more seriously about the course, to read through the texts, and to try to make plans, especially for setting up the group projects. I read Michael Rost's *Listening in Language Learning* (1990) and was particularly interested in the following sections, which I copied in my teaching journal:

Two questions emerge that are important for pedagogy. How can the learner find useful comparisons between their current interpretations and responses to the L2 event and those which might be more favourable, or "acceptable"? How can the learners increase the quality of their interpretations and responses? (155) Outcomes allow learners to make their interpretations tangible and thereby make comparisons between their current interpretations and those of the instructor or of other learners, or their own own later (and earlier) responses on the same task. (168) Only by realizing possible causes of misunderstandings and non-understandings that lead to partially acceptable outcomes can the instructor draw attention to strategies for re-understanding the task. (169)

From the ideas in this section, I began to think that one primary goal of the course would be to increase learner responsibility for understanding, to have some sort of sequence in which students could demonstrate what they had understood, ask questions about what they hadn't, and then reflect on what they had learned both about the culture and the language. I drew one of my first mindmaps for the course and listed four objectives: increasing students' listening comprehension, increasing learner responsibility for understanding, learning the language through listening, and learning about contemporary lifestyles and issues in the United Kingdom and the United States. Some topic areas that I thought might be important were multi-cultural society, female and male roles and relationships, education, changes in family structure, and social problems. These were all topics I was interested in and had been chosen as research topics by my seminar students in previous years.

My next task was to write my start-of-the-year letter to students, describing the course and my expectations. In my other courses, this letter is usually an odd mixture of cheery encouragement ("Welcome to Oral English I") and subtle threat ("If you want to pass, you had better . . ."), but for this elective course, I toned down the threats and emphasized that we would be working together to create an exciting new course and that my main role would be as resource person and guide (see Appendix A). I stated that the two goals of the course would be learning how to learn through listening and increasing understanding of life in the English-speaking countries. I gave four requirements for satisfactorily completing the course: attendance and punctuality, completing the homework assignments, keeping a daily listening diary, and doing a group project each semester.

I spent a lot of time thinking about how to set up the group projects, and in the letter, I explained in great detail what the projects involved, the planning and presentation procedure students were to follow, and the kind of group project proposal they were to write. Each group would select a listening material related to one topic area of the course and design a listening task for that material. In their project presentation, they would introduce the material, explain the listening task, have the other students do the task, give feedback, and answer any questions on the material. Each group would hand in their proposal at the beginning of the course so that I could give feedback and suggestions, prevent duplication of material, and arrange an appropriate schedule. With thirty-eight students, I figured I would have nine or ten groups, and with only thirteen classes per semester, I realized I needed to get the students started right away on planning their projects so that we could have one per class.

I have spent quite a lot of time planning the first day and am still not sure exactly what I am going to do. I made a form for students to write down their goals, the topic areas they are interested in, and the kinds of materials they would like to use. Considering that the students have thought about these questions in writing their essays, though that was back in November, I am hopeful that it won't take them too long to fill out the form. Next I'll have them discuss in groups of four to find the most popular choices, put those on the board, and have them vote. Then I'll have them stand up and form groups, using the choices with the most votes, first by goal, then by topic, and finally, by material, and I hope they will be able to find people with similar interests to form their project groups. This is where I am now, the Sunday before classes start. In thinking about what I've written so far, I can see that in my approach to course design, I put a lot more emphasis on process than content, on setting systems in motion.

Well, classes have definitely begun – so much for all those brave initial plans! Now I'm full of questions about what to do and planning the course week by week. My teaching journal entry after the first day of class begins, "*Oh, No*! I'm afraid I've rushed them into the group projects. Some students may feel insecure and overwhelmed and never return." I soon realized as the students were rushing around the language lab to form and re-form groups that I should have given them the form for homework and done the talking and mixing in the second class, even if it meant some difficulties in scheduling the group projects. I guess I was too obsessed with my "brilliant" idea.

I have decided that I'll use *How to Listen* and half of *Adrian Mole* this semester. I thought it would be better to begin with *How to Listen* so that students could learn the strategies and apply them in their class and homework listening. Another part of their strategy training is having students read others' listening diaries when I collect them at the end of the month and reflect on what they learned from reading the other diaries. In my work with the *Adrian Mole* video, I'm using some of Sherraid Scott's (1991) ideas for video activities, having students write summaries together and think of questions in small groups, as a way of applying Rost's (1990) concept of making comparisons between interpretations. Usually, after the first video viewing, I have the students work together in groups of four to ask questions about the story, culture, and vocabulary of the episode. Several members of the class took a college study trip to England, so I usually try to have them answer students' questions first. Sometimes I'll give my interpretation, reminding them that I am not a native of the United Kingdom either, or I'll tell them to try to answer the questions after a second viewing in class or after listening to the audio tape at home. Students can also view the video in the college audio-visual center as often as they like, and I was quite impressed when one student made a transcription of the video as part of her listening diary work.

I'm feeling a little confused about having created too broad a canvas for my context. It's rich, but is it deep? From our first-day debacle emerged five important topic areas for our work this year: family life, education, racial discrimination, work, and religion and values. I like the idea of having a feast in which each student can have a different experience of the course, but are there too many dishes on the table? For their projects, students have chosen movie scenes from *Kramer vs. Kramer* and *Baby Boom,* songs such as "Across the Lines," and various other materials.

I read Peter Elbow's (1986) essay on competency-based learning and like him began to wonder, Is it all right to pursue the inquiry process without clear and specific knowledge and skill goals? I'm worried that things are going to get fuzzy and disjointed. Yet how can I say exactly what I want the students to learn when they have such a variety of interests, background knowledge, experience, and language skills? The competencies I have in mind relate more to the kinds of learners I hope my students will become: listening learners who have goals, are able to select materials and use effective strategies to reach those goals, and are able to evaluate their own progress and, in terms of culture learning, learners who have questions about contemporary lifestyles and develop schemata to fit in new information. I feel like I'm leaping off, not knowing exactly what to expect or where we will all land in January, when the course ends.

June 19

Advanced listening is turning out to be an exciting class. I'm learning a lot from teaching an elective, though it has been a bittersweet learning experience. I often feel out of control. I can't make the students come to class, I can't make them do their homework, I don't know how the groups will do with their projects, I can't even be sure the lab will work as I make new mistakes each week. But somehow, at the beginning of June, I suddenly got the feeling of being freed. "I don't have to *make* them study – they are happy to do it on their own. And I am free to enjoy my role as resource person." The course has become a kind of Counseling Learning or Community Language Learning (Curran 1976) of listening, emphasizing student choice and investment with me as cultural and linguistic informant, a very comfortable teaching role.

In general, I have divided the class into three time segments, with the first thirty minutes devoted to going over the homework from *How to Listen,* the second thirty minutes to the group project of the week, and the final thirty minutes to watching and discussing *Adrian Mole.* I am enjoying this video, which has turned out to be a great choice because although I hadn't realized it when I selected it, the book and video are a social and political satire on Thatcher's England and fit in perfectly with the content of the course. The video is full of sly British humor, which means that *I* can watch it a million times and not get bored. But it can also be taken simply as the story of a young British boy growing up. The material is difficult, though, and this is also a problem with *How to Listen* – advanced listening indeed, whereas most of the students are at the intermediate level. Students are not doing the homework for *How to Listen* which is a bad sign, although there is evidence of strategy use in some students' listening diaries. I try to be sure to cover the strategies in class so that even if the students aren't listening to the tape, they'll be getting some ideas about listening strategies.

The quality of the group project presentations has varied, but in general, the student presenters have done a good job and the other students have listened attentively as the presenters explained how the material related to our topic areas and have worked hard on the listening task. Usually, the presenters did their own transcription, which I checked, and then they prepared a handout with fill-in-the-blanks and a few comprehension questions. This intensive listening work has given a good balance to our class listening activities as the *Adrian Mole* activities are of a more global nature.

I'm thinking now about the questions I want to ask for the first semester evaluation class and self-evaluations (see Appendix B). How do students like doing the group projects? Do they want to continue them? What do they think about the materials? How would they evaluate their own work? What would they like to do in the fall semester? For their summer vacation homework, I'll have them continue their listening diaries, try out the strategy training activities from the listening diary program, and finish *How to Listen.*

September 2

Second semester starts in a couple of weeks, so it's time to assess advanced listening, first on my own and then by reading and reflecting on the student evaluations. Only ten students of the twenty-eight or so remaining in class handed in evaluations, so I won't be able to get a full view, but this seems to be how it goes with elective courses. In some ways, it's a relief. For example, in my required Oral English II class, all but one or two of the twenty-six students hand in their listening diaries every month, and it takes several hours to go through them and give feedback, so I'm secretly quite pleased when I get a small harvest of listening diaries in advanced listening.

My reflections on the course have been influenced by my preparations for a special course I'll be teaching for the alumni, Looking at the Language Learning Process, which will meet once a month for five months. I plan to have the participants design and carry out a language-learning project for the five months of the course. In reviewing the resource books on learner training, I began to think it would be a good idea to take this component of the listening diary program for advanced listening a step further and have students plan and carry out a long-term listening project as part of their listening diary homework this semester. My hope is that this experience will motivate them to continue and prepare them to organize their listening study after graduation, as Ms. Miyabe, the graduate who inspired my master's research (Fujiwara 1990), has done. I have been thinking of how to set up these projects and how to have students with common interests share ideas. I'll have students reflect on the listening diary work they have done so far and particularly on the training activities they did over the summer. I also want students to form new groups for their group projects, though remembering my first-day debacle, I'll stretch these organizing activities over a few classes and give students more time to reflect, form groups, and discuss.

I'm still struggling with basic questions on my approach to the course. I think five topics were too many, although the students' July mindmaps on contemporary lifestyles and issues, compared to their April ones, showed that they had learned a lot about the course content during the semester. In the second semester, I want to try to tighten the context and make better use of the discussion and processing time.

I also want to do more experimentation with active strategy training. The problem is that except for inferencing and questioning, I have a hard time remembering the strategies myself (and I wrote a thesis on them!). I thought *How to Listen* was going to take care of the strategy training for me, but I'm afraid the book was too difficult and that not many students actually did enough of the homework to get the benefit of the training. Maybe I should think about writing an intermediate-level listening text that would have one content area (deep and rich, of course!) and strategy training. That would be a real challenge! It would probably be a good idea to reflect on how I learn from listening as a foreign language learner of Japanese. In my own learning, as in my teaching, I prefer the intuitive to the organized approach. Probably what I should do next year is just take strategies from *How to Listen* and the Oxford (1990) and O'Malley and Chamot (1990) books and try to apply them to *Adrian Mole* and *Talk Radio* rather than having *How to Listen,* too. Perhaps by reviewing and applying the strategies, I can internalize them and use them naturally in my teaching.

Of the ten students who handed in their evaluations, nine were very positive about the group projects. Seven thought *Adrian Mole* was a good material, whereas only four thought *How to Listen* was. Several students commented that the class was very different from LL and that they liked the emphasis on student choice and initiative. One said she preferred the individual study style of LL, and another said she wanted to have quizzes every week like they did in LL. I had debated whether to have quizzes or not, but besides not having mastered the quiz feedback technology of the lab, I wanted to get away from the idea of studying for points, of listening to pass quizzes rather than listening for one's own learning.

One student said her goal was to understand authentic materials at natural speed, which I recall was what a lot of students had said in their original essays. Is this a feasible goal in a year? How can I break this goal down into more manageable steps or areas? Just as reading in one content area could move a student through the Chall (1983) stages of reading development, can listening in one content area move a student to advanced proficiency, and would this be applicable across topics and situations? It doesn't seem to be the case in my own learning of Japanese, where I have near-native understanding in some situations and on some topics but flounder pitifully in others.

November 20

Things are going quite well in advanced listening this semester. I have kept the same basic pattern of class activities, going over the homework on *Talk Radio* in the first third of class, then focusing on the group project of the week, and finally, watching and processing *Adrian Mole*. I have accepted the fact that there will be disparities in the amount of homework the students do and have decided that as far as grading is concerned, those students who come fairly regularly will pass and whatever work students have done will add points to their grade with no penalties for work not done. So I take a businesslike approach in correcting the homework, quickly passing over the students who haven't done it that week. Actually, though, more students are doing the homework for *Talk Radio* and so am I, (I don't have a teacher's manual at home). The content of the talk shows is quite interesting, and because it's my own culture, I feel on safer ground adding information and insights.

Talk Radio has two tapes, one of the actual talk show conversations, with two callers per topic, and one tape, *Focus on Vocabulary,* which has two sample sentences of the more difficult words and phrases, one taken from the conversations but recorded slowly and clearly. The vocabulary tape has provided an important crutch for the weaker students, and some of them begin with this tape rather than the conversations. As we go over the vocabulary exercises, I read the sentences again for those students who didn't do their homework or couldn't guess the definitions. I've been surprised and, I must admit, a little irritated by students' reluctance to guess at meanings, especially considering that the second sample sentence is practically a definition. I know only too well that this reluctance to guess is part of Japanese school culture, but its persistence among my rather lively and sophisticated learners puzzles me. "Guessing is a very important strategy," I intone, and some class members, especially those who have studied abroad, will try, but others steadfastly refuse. Why? What should I do?

I took time in the first three classes to set up the group projects and long-term listening diary projects. I was glad when the students chose only four of the five original topic areas. Maybe that will tighten things up a bit. I was surprised and a little chagrined that none of the students chose ESP audio courses in secretarial and business English for their individual projects, although I have been steadily ordering them for the audiovisual center. Why not? Wouldn't these be good career preparation? Their choice of materials, in order of popularity, were movies, books on tape, academic listening,

English language teaching (ELT) videos, and songs. I had them discuss materials and strategies in groups, and I went around to each group and shared my knowledge of the audiovisual center's resources.

I have been quite impressed this semester with the students' group projects, both with their ability to choose relevant materials and the professional way in which they have prepared listening tasks and handouts. For example, the group that was interested in religion and values chose the scenes from *Hannah and Her Sisters* in which Woody Allen, who is contemplating converting from Judaism to Catholicism, talks to a Catholic priest and then visits his parents to tell them of his desire. This group asked me to correct their transcription, and I was amazed at how well they had done, as Woody Allen speaks at such an incredible speed that *I* had a hard time completing their transcription. Another group chose a wedding preparation scene from the ELT video, *Family Album,* which to me seemed an example of "linguistically antiseptic and emotionally sterile" (Stevick 1980: 203) ELT materials, although many students found it interesting. The contrast between the linguistic and cultural complexity and emotional drama of the family scene in *Hannah and Her Sisters* and the cheerful, rather atypically functional family life of *Family Album* was revealing and amusing.

The quotes from Michael Rost that I had written in my teaching journal months ago took on a living dimension with the scene from *Hannah and Her Sisters.* Though I made some remarks after the group project, I had no idea how to transfer or even share my understanding of the dense cultural information contained in the scene and, particularly, the humor ("I'll dye Easter eggs, whatever it takes," Woody says to the priest) with my Japanese students. After class, one student thanked me for my remarks because she said she finally understood why her Jewish host mother in Australia hadn't sent her a Christmas card back. This is what she got out of the group project, and it was important for her. Did any students arrive at an "acceptable" (Rost 1990: 155) interpretation, one that a native speaker would have? Which native speaker? A New York Jew and a Texas Baptist might have two very different interpretations of the scene, just as I'm sure a British person would pick up many more subtle nuances of accent, and culture in *Adrian Mole* than I have been able to do. When this particular group had originally told me they wanted to do a movie scene on the topic of religion and asked me for suggestions, I was at a loss. *The Bells of St. Mary's*? Recent movies on religion? Nothing came to mind.

What I realized from this incident and similar ones is that we can rely on the genius of the learner. Dean Barnlund (1991), in one of his seminars on intercultural communication, said that he has his graduate students choose thesis topics on some aspect of a different culture that had surprised or interested them and that these aspects usually turn out to be rich research topics. Similarly, having the students choose materials, an idea reached in desperation, has turned out to be very fruitful, as most groups have chosen materials full of cultural information – cultural holograms, so to speak. Perhaps there is method in this inquiry process madness after all.

May 2

There are many questions on my mind as I begin my second year teaching advanced listening. I regret that I haven't put enough time and thought into replanning the course because I have two new courses to design and teach this year and I was busy planning them during spring vacation and working on a couple of papers. Actually, if I didn't have to write this chapter, I would have coasted through the first month at least!

However, I have been thinking about various issues concerned with the course because I had to rework my JALT '91 presentation, "Learner Training in Listening Strategies," for the Kyoto chapter presentation I gave last week, and I wrote a paper on the Looking at the Language Learning Process course I taught to our alumni last fall. I have also been reading some books and articles on women's studies and education for my new courses. In doing all this, I began to rediscover the various theoretical and experiential strands that are woven into the advanced listening course. It's amazing how one reads and attends presentations in certain areas and absorbs concepts and techniques that are then "forgotten," so that when asked, "Why are you teaching this way?" one lapses into inarticulateness. But for a while, at least, I'll be able to answer, "Well, I designed the course this way because of my study of the comprehension approach (Winitz 1981), good learner research (Stern 1975), learner training (Wenden and Rubin 1987), and content-based language instruction (Mohan 1986) and because of my belief in a rich and deep context for learning and the "mid-wife" (Belenky, Clinchy, Goldberger, and Tarule 1986) counseling (Curran 1976) approach to education. I'm feeling an intellectual pleasure and pride in having unwoven the threads of my teaching fabric.

I have even traced my interest in listening back to *Cheaper by the Dozen,* a book of my childhood. The efficiency expert father has his numerous children listen to foreign language tapes while they are in the bathtub and is then quite discomfited when they begin to speak French at the dinner table and he can't understand. I wonder if *Cheaper by the Dozen* was the genesis of my own preference as a learner for the comprehension approach or if it's because I have the linguistic intelligence postulated by Gardner (1983) in his theory of multiple intelligences. In any case, when doing my mindmap for the Kyoto presentation, I realized that I may emphasize inference and discovery in my class because I often find the experience of being a listening learner very exhilarating. I have to remember my bias in this area and consider that for some people, learning a foreign language through listening (Nida 1957) provokes the same anxiety and reluctance that learning how to use the language lab causes in me.

In December, I asked for feedback on the materials, and we had a class discussion in which it soon became clear that *How to Listen* would have to go. Although the more sophisticated students realized the value of strategy training, almost of all of the students felt that the material was too difficult and (the fatal blow!) boring. The topics of the tape extracts, even within units, were often unrelated, and the lack of context made the high-speed short talks by professional BBC announcers very hard for students to understand. Moreover, the students found the topics unrelated to our course themes or to their own lives, whereas the equally difficult *Talk Radio* had real conversations on topics they were interested in and there were two callers for each topic, which provided more context. I felt that part of the reaction to *How to Listen* may have been caused by my less than skillful use of the book. But I had to admit that in terms of my own belief in a rich, deep context, the students' criticisms were sound and in fact, true of many of the materials now on the market that take the "sound bite" approach. *Adrian Mole,* of course, had a story line and characters to hold it together, and the students found it difficult but interesting and "friendly." I am not sure how many students realized that it was a satire, but the fact that it could be taken on many levels made it a rich and deep context for discovery.

I reread parts of *Listening in Language Learning* (Rost 1990), and the balloon of intellectual pride that I had been feeling quickly deflated as I realized how elementary my understanding of the listening process still is. Rost discusses a "layered" approach to developing language skills, and I think this was the import of the feedback several students gave. One student suggested that there should be different levels of exercises for the different levels of students in the class. Three other students recommended that I use a more step-by-step approach, and another suggested that I give more information and guidance when viewing the video. My strength as a teacher is to stress discovery, but my weakness is that sometimes I don't give enough support for the discovery process, so I need to work on providing the right amount of support. This year, as we will have only two main materials and I will be more familiar with them, I can work on providing support by taking more time to understand students' interpretations of the materials and experimenting with ways to help them "increase the quality of their interpretations" (Rost 1990: 155).

One interesting thing that came out in the feedback from my final course evaluation (see Appendix C) was how much the students learned from each other, not only from the group projects but just from the stimulation of being with a motivated and active group of learners. Judging from their essays and our first two classes, this year's group seems even more motivated and sophisticated, and I think they will act as "worthy rivals" for one another, as one student put it in her essay. I was rather taken aback in our first class when they did their initial project brainstorming and came up with AIDS, homosexuality, and murder (lifestyle? issue?). I felt the need for a little emotional sterility and said, "Aren't these topics a little heavy? They're OK, of course, if that's what you want to study, but I think more general topics might be better." I was relieved when the final choices in the next class were family problems, the class system of the British Isles, and youth culture and pleased that with only three topics, there would be more depth to our study.

A feast with materials for discovery is the way I have conceived of this course, and another interesting feature of the student feedback was the variety in significant points of culture learning and changes in students' approaches to listening. Of the fourteen students who handed in evaluations, seven found school life a significant topic area; six, divorce; four, comparison of cultural values; three, unemployment; two, racial discrimination; two, religion; and one each, family life, working women in the United States, and food. In terms of improving their listening comprehension and strategies, three students cited each of the following changes: their comprehension had greatly improved; their attitude toward listening had become more positive; they had learned to pay attention to key points; they had improved their ability to understand the whole story in one viewing; and they had built up their vocabulary. Two reported that they were better able to imagine the outline of the story. One had improved her ability to analyze various aspects, including linguistic and cultural; one guessed words more; one used repeated listening more; one had improved in dictating words; and one was now able to understand the lines in movies. This variety and specificity seemed to confirm that the true syllabus of this course is the spiral of growing independence, curiosity, and depth of cultural understanding, which is different for each learner in the class.

Appendix A: Letter with precourse information for students

Dear Students,

Welcome to our course in *advanced listening!* I am very excited about this course for a number of reasons. First of all, this is the first year that this course will be given, and I think we have a big challenge and responsibility to create an interesting and significant course together. I have read your essays several times, and I think all of you have worthwhile goals and good ideas for accomplishing those goals.

Second, from my own experience as a language learner and teacher, I firmly believe that listening practice is the key to language learning. An important part of your work in this course will be learning how to learn through listening and sharing your ideas about the process with your classmates.

Another major goal of this course is to learn about contemporary life-styles and issues in the United States and the United Kingdom. Therefore, as you improve your listening comprehension, you will also increase your understanding of life in these English-speaking countries.

You will be able to make many choices concerning your own listening study in accordance with your personal goals. I will act as a resource person and guide, and I hope you will find many helpful partners and worthy rivals among the other students in the class.

To complete the course satisfactorily, you must do the following:

1. Attend every class and be on time.
2. Complete all homework assignments.
3. Keep a listening diary. I expect you to listen to English at least 20 to 30 minutes every day and to keep a record of your work. I recommend that you listen to a variety of materials and try to keep a balance among the different kinds. You can use our course materials, the audiovisual center's self-study materials, English songs, TV programs and movies. Please keep this journal on binder loose-leaf paper, and hand it in at the end of every month. Write the following for each daily entry:
   (a) Date and the time you began and finished
   (b) Kinds of materials and titles
   (c) Your listening strategies, reactions, and questions
   (d) What you learned from your listening
4. Complete a group project. In groups of three, you will take responsibility for choosing the material and designing the listening task for one class. (See details below.)

Group Project

Each semester, you will make a 20- to 30-minute group presentation in which you will teach a listening material of your choice. The material should be 2 to 3 minutes in length and should relate to one of the themes the class has chosen. The material can be a song, TV or movie scene, textbook lesson, or something else. However, you cannot use materials with Japanese subtitles or English captions. You must give me a copy of the audio or video cassette and your handout a week before your presentation.

Presentation Format
1. Briefly introduce the material, explaining why you are interested in it and what aspect of contemporary life it shows.
2. Explain the learning task. You play the tape, and students do the learning task.
3. Give feedback on the activity, and answer any questions about the material.

Preparation
Choose the material and time it. Decide on the listening task, and prepare a handout with the task and any necessary vocabulary definitions. Make a copy of the material, and hand in the tape and handout a week in advance. Prepare your introduction, and listen to the material several times so that you know it very well and can explain it to others. Ask me if you have any questions.

Group Project Proposal
Prepare two choices in case another group selects the same material.

1. What material are you going to use?
2. Why are you interested in this material?
3. What kind of listening task will you do?

I'm looking forward to a very busy and active class!

Sincerely yours,

Appendix B: Midterm evaluation and homework assignment

Advanced Listening

Dear Students,

I would like to thank you for your participation and cooperation this semester. I have greatly enjoyed creating our Advanced Listening course together with you. You have selected very interesting materials for your group projects and I think they have given us important insights into contemporary issues and lifestyles in the United States and the United Kingdom. I would especially like to thank you for your patience with my problems in using the language lab.

In this letter, I would like to explain about our interview project, your evaluation, and your summer homework. I know you will have very busy summers, but I would like you to continue your daily listening practice so that you can maintain and further improve your listening ability.

Interview Questions

As I mentioned before, Prof. Edasawa will be traveling to England this summer and I will be traveling to the United States. If possible, we will try to interview people on topics that interest you and record these interviews so that we can listen to them in the second semester. Therefore, I would like you to think of three to five questions about contemporary lifestyles and issues in each country, and we will use these questions for our interviews. For the questions on the United Kingdom, look through your notes on *Adrian Mole* and choose the questions that you find most interesting. For the questions on the United States, think about what you've learned from the group projects and other materials.

Class and Self-evaluation

As we end our first semester, I would like you to reflect on your work for this course and evaluate how you have studied and what you have learned. I would also like you to give me your honest feedback and opinions about the class, as they will help me in planning the second semester.

1. What do you think about our Advanced Listening class?
2. What is your opinion of the main materials, *The Secret Diary of Adrian Mole* and *How to Listen*? What have you learned from them?
3. What do think about the group projects? What have you learned from them?
4. How would you evaluate your classwork, homework, and group project?

5. What are your listening goals now? What do you need to do to achieve them?

6. How and what would you like to study in this class second semester?

"How to Listen"

During the vacation, I would like you to finish our text, *How to Listen.* You can use it as one of the materials for your listening diary. After you complete a lesson, you can check your answers against the Answer Key on pages 101–109. If you want to try doing dictations of some of the extracts, you can check your work against the transcripts on pages 69–99. You can learn many helpful listening strategies from *How to Listen,* and I suggest that you experiment with these strategies when you use other materials.

Summer Homework

Your summer homework is to continue your listening diary throughout the summer, except for the exam period. Try to listen to a well-balanced variety of materials. In the comments section, in addition to your reactions and questions, please write about what you have learned from your listening. You may write about general points (pronunciation, word linking, accents, conversational style) or give specific words or expressions you learned. I would like you to choose four of the following activities and try each one a few times during the vacation. Some of the activities may take more than one day, but you should record your work or your comments in your listening diary *every* day.

Sounds: Choose one or two sounds whose pronunciation you want to improve. Listen to a song several times, and write down all the words with the sounds you have chosen. Check your guesses by looking at the lyrics. How did you do?

Conversation: From a movie or TV program you like, record a 1- or 2-minute scene in which two people are talking. Describe the people, their relationship, and the situation. Then transcribe their conversation. What interesting things did you notice or learn about interaction in English?

English News: Watch the news, and write down the main topics discussed. Choose one topic, and write down some words you remembered or learned while watching the broadcast. Experiment with different strategies for watching the news: Watch the news in Japanese before or after the English news; read an English newspaper and look up the new words before watching; follow a particular topic for several days. How do the different strategies help you understand the news?

Interview: Listen to or watch an interview in English. What did you learn about the life or ideas of the person being interviewed? What questions did the interviewer ask?

Tourist Information: Call either the Kyoto (075-361-2911) or Nara (0742-27-1313) tourist information recording, and take notes on the main events. Check your notes with the newspaper or the Japanese recording. What helped you understand the main ideas?

Books on Tape: Listen to a tape of a book or story, and summarize what happens and what you think will happen. What do you imagine about the characters and scenes of the story?

I also recommend that you try listening to materials from the audiovisual center, either the self-study program or some of the videos and audiocassettes made especially for English study. Recommended videos are *A Weekend Away, Mystery Tour, Person to Person, Favourite Fairy Tales, Video English 1* and *2,* and *At Home in Britain.* Recommended audiocassettes are *Small Talk, Jazz Chants, Yoshi Goes to New York,* and textbook tapes from the other Oral English classes.

Sincerely yours,

Appendix C: Final course evaluation

Dear Advanced Listening Students,

As we come to the end of our course, I would like you to reflect on what you have learned this year and how you have learned it. The evaluation process is important for a number of reasons. Thinking about your learning process helps you consolidate what you learned this year and prepare you for studying on your own after graduation. I will use your self-evaluation to determine your final grade and will use your feedback on the course to plan for next year. Feel free to organize your evaluation in the way that seems best to you, but please cover the following areas.

Self-Evaluation

Content: What were the most significant things you learned about contemporary issues and lifestyles in the United Kingdom and the United States? Why? What were the most interesting? Why? What would you like to learn more about? How can you continue your study?

Listening: How has your listening ability changed since April? How has you approach to listening changed? What are your strengths and weaknesses as a listening learner? What kind of listening program do you plan for yourself after graduation? What goals do you hope to achieve?

Coursework: Describe and evaluate your classwork, homework, and work for the two group projects. What do you feel proudest of? What do you regret?

Course Evaluation

What class and homework activities did you find most helpful? Why? Most interesting? Why? Least helpful? Least enjoyable? Why?

What did you think about this course in general? Did it meet your expectations? Why or why not?

What suggestions do you have to improve this course?

Any other comments?

Materials

(Those who turned in evaluations can skip this part.)

What did you think about the three main materials for this course?

Sincerely yours,

ANALYSIS AND TASKS

Barbara Fujiwara's course is being held not because there is a gap in the students' skills that must be bridged in order for them to succeed in a certain context but because students have expressed a desire to continue a course of study, in this case, listening comprehension. Though Fujiwara can assume that her students have the desire to become better listeners, it is up to her to determine what kind of progress they should make and how. She will have to determine the students' shortcomings with respect to listening and how to overcome them. Fujiwara's approach to this task is consonant with her beliefs about learning: that each group of students has diverse needs that they can individually identify and develop strategies to meet.

In conceptualizing the course, Fujiwara thinks in terms of what she wants the students to do both in and out of class – as she puts it, the "activities and visions" of the class. These activities derive from techniques she has used in the past, how she views her role and that of the students, and ideas from other teachers. The activities are grounded in three considerations or goals, two based on theories of learning – students as independent learners and the need for content to provide a deep, rich context – and one pragmatic – keeping students in the course and thereby keeping the course in the curriculum.

An important factor for Fujiwara is that what students do in and out of class should be an example of what they can do on their own, without the structure of a course. Thus obtaining input from the students, offering them choices, and having them take the teacher's role are important features of her course design. Making her expectations of the students clear to them is an essential step in the realization of this approach.

For Fujiwara, the key to the success of the course seems to be finding the right materials, the criterion being that they help achieve the goals. She must first decide whether to develop her own materials or to use published works. She opts for the latter because of time constraints. She is able to find core materials but is concerned about finding and developing the supplementary materials that are to provide the variety she sees as necessary in meeting students' diverse needs. She decides to have the students themselves provide the variety by working in groups to find their own materials and prepare presentations based on them.

Reflection plays an important role in Fujiwara's process and takes many forms: a teaching journal, reflection on what she has read, mindmaps to help her conceptualize what she is doing. The influences of others, both her colleagues and readings on listening theory, play a role in shaping her thinking and her practice. Throughout the development of the course, Fujiwara tries to apply theory that has made sense to her and to gain a greater understanding of it from her practice. She does this both consciously and intuitively. For example, she determines what her main objectives are after reflecting on something she has read and drawing a mindmap to help her conceptualize why it is important to her.

Changes in the course come about in response to feedback she solicits from students as well as her observations of what was effective in meeting the goals and what wasn't. The second time she teaches the course, she decides to drop one of the books. She realizes that even though the book seems to fit her goal of having students develop strategies to become independent listeners, in practice it doesn't help students meet the goal because most find it too difficult and consequently don't do the work. This is an example of how a choice made on principle can fail to work in practice.

One of Fujiwara's main quandaries about this type of course is whether or not the lack of "clear and specific knowledge and skill goals" is a hindrance to learning. She counters this with the consideration that the competencies she has in mind "relate more to the kinds of learners I hope my students will become" and to the question "How can I say exactly what I want the students to learn when they have such a variety of interests, background knowledge, experience, and language skills?" This dilemma remains a source of creative tension throughout the course.

FOCUS ON SELECTING AND DEVELOPING MATERIALS AND ACTIVITIES AND ORGANIZATION OF CONTENT AND ACTIVITIES

1. Fujiwara used two of her goals as guides in deciding on materials to use in her course: whether they provided explicit guidance in how to develop learning strategies and whether they were content-based.

   Review your goals and objectives. On what basis have you chosen the material for your course? Will the material enable you to fulfill those goals?

   If you do not choose your own materials but are working with a prescribed text, for example, list some ways you can adapt it so that it will help fulfill your goals for the course.

2. A key consideration for Fujiwara in planning and organizing her course was her own role and that of her students. She saw her role as that of resource and guide, and so the success of the course depended on her students' input and willingness to take an active part in class and also outside of class through homework assignments such as listening diaries. She decided to devote one third of each class to in-class presentations by students, which they had prepared in small groups. Students

were informed of the presentations by letter, and much time in the first classes was devoted to forming groups.

- Consider your own course. What kind of input and participation do you expect from your students? How will this influence the way you organize the course? Are your expectations realistic, given who your students are and other constraints and resources?
- Write a letter to your students in which you introduce your objectives, your intended organization of the course and reasons for it, and your expectations of the class members.
- Consider the first day of class. How will you introduce your way of working? What will you do on the first day to set the tone of the course?

3. Fujiwara talks about the importance of setting systems in motion, mechanisms that will provide structure and continuity for the course. Involving students in selecting topics, having them prepare and present listening activities, segmenting each class into three parts, and having students keep listening diaries are all examples of systems in Fujiwara's sense.

   Consider your own course. What systems can you establish? How will you communicate them to your students?

4. Ongoing reflection and assessment – taking time to think about the course – played an important role in Fujiwara's development of her course and took a variety of forms: keeping a teaching journal, reflecting on conversations with colleagues, copying down quotes about listening theory and reflecting on how such theory might be implemented in her course, making mindmaps, writing this chapter.

   List the ways you allow yourself to reflect and assess as you plan and teach your course. Which are most productive for you? Why?

5. Fujiwara noted that she was significantly influenced by some reading about listening theory. The theory helped her set objectives and gave her a lens for viewing certain class activities. She also came to question some of the theory after having taught the class.

   List specific ideas or statements you think are important concerning what you are going to teach in your course and how you are going to teach it. Describe how those ideas have manifested themselves in the design of your course.

6. One way Fujiwara involved her students in her course planning was through feedback questionnaires given in the middle and at the end of the course. The feedback caused her to alter some aspects of her course.

   Review Appendixes B and C. Are such questionnaires suitable for your course? How would you change them to suit your course and why? What other feedback mechanisms could you use to get input from your students regarding the effectiveness of the course?

References

Barnlund, D. 1991, March. Teaching Intercultural Communication. Seminar, Kyoto, Japan.

Belenky, M., B. Clinchy, N. Goldberger, and J. Tarule. 1986. *Women's Ways of Knowing: The Development of Self, Voice, and Mind.* New York: Basic Books.

Chall, J. 1983. *Stages of Reading Development.* NewYork: McGraw-Hill.

Curran, C. 1976. *Counseling-Learning in Second Languages.* Apple River, Ill.: Apple River Press.

Elbow, P. 1986. *Embracing Contraries: Explorations in Learning and Teaching.* New York: Oxford University Press.

Fujiwara, B. 1990. Learner training in listening strategies. *JALT Journal 12* (2): 203–217.

Gardner, H. 1983. *Frames of Mind: The Theory of Multiple Intelligences.* New York: Basic Books.

Geddes, M. 1988. *How to Listen: An Intermediate Course in Listening Skills.* Oxford: BBC English.

Mohan, B. 1986. *Language and Content.* Reading, Mass.: Addison-Wesley.

Nida, E. 1957. *Learning a Foreign Language.* New York: Friendship Press.

O'Malley, J. M., and A. U. Chamot. 1990. *Learning Strategies in Second Language Acquisition.* New York: Cambridge University Press.

Oxford, R. 1990. *Language Learning Strategies: What Every Teacher Should Know.* Rowley, Mass.: Newbury House.

Rost, M. 1990. *Listening in Language Learning.* London: Longman.

Sadow, C., and E. Sather. 1987. *Talk Radio.* Reading, Mass.: Addison-Wesley.

Scott, S. 1991. Rings. *Aichi Junior College Research Papers 14:* 1–18.

Stern, H. H. 1975. What can we learn from the good language learner? *Canadian Modern Language Review 31:* 304–318.

Stevick, E. 1980. *A Way and Ways.* Rowley, Mass.: Newbury House.

Wenden, A. L., and Rubin, J., eds. 1987. *Learning Strategies in Language Learning.* Englewood Cliffs, N.J.: Prentice Hall.

Winitz, H., ed. 1981. *The Comprehension Approach to Foreign Language Instruction.* Rowley, Mass.: Newbury House.

8 A curriculum framework for corporate language programs

Laura Hull

Laura Hull's teaching experience in academic English, intensive English, and English for special purposes programs spans both ESL and EFL settings. She has been an administrator, curriculum designer, and staff developer for language programs and community service programs such as Hospice. She has been involved in designing and teaching courses for business personnel in the United States for more than six years. The experience she describes here occurred over a period of a year and involved developing a curriculum framework for an existing program of loosely related courses for corporate executives from Asia, Latin America, and Europe.

The course development focus for this chapter is evaluation. Consider the following questions as you read:

Whose needs and expectations did Hull take into account in evaluating the existing program?
How does the framework assist in reconciling the various needs?

Curriculum development process

The call came late in the day on a Thursday. Could I coteach a corporate tutorial starting on Monday? There was an emergency – the instructor who was to do the whole tutorial had a scheduling conflict – and a split tutorial for this corporate student was the best solution. I would teach in the afternoons. The student was a middle manager in a pharmaceutical company who needed to work on some basic language and presentation skills before a series of important meetings at his U.S. corporate headquarters, where he would be presenting proposals to senior management. This person's first language was Japanese. That was virtually all that I knew before my arrival in the classroom Monday afternoon.

My orientation to the corporate language program delivery system had been cursory; the time for planning minimal; the instructor in the morning tutorial unknown to me; and the curriculum guidelines virtually nonexistent. In spite of these obstacles, the other instructor and I cobbled together a program of sorts for this eight-week tutorial, seeking to find learning activities that would help the student meet his goals and objectives. These goals and objectives were stated in broad terms that made their measurability challenging. Yet we were to be held accountable, we were told, by the client company for the achievement of those goals.

Our experience in other areas of ESL teaching helped us design a program that was satisfactory for the student. Indeed, I found later that it was the excellence of the training provided by individual instructors that had built the reputation that the corporate language programs currently enjoyed. However, the cost – in planning time, in frustration at not having clear guidelines for course content, in uncertainty that the program would in fact meet the needs of the student and fulfill the expectations of the sponsoring corporation – was high.

Background

Later that year, in the early summer, I became the director of these corporate language programs. My contract stipulated that I would also be an instructor when the administrative demands of the programs allowed. Although corporate language programs was not a new department, it had not been in the forefront of the institution's language-learning program offerings until the past year. With the recognition that English language training for business executives was a profitable and fast-developing field, more attention was being paid to marketing and to the service delivery of these programs. The approach of the institution was to provide personalized language-learning programs to meet the needs of corporate clients and the students they sent for training whenever the client requested. In other words, there would not be regularly scheduled intake periods throughout the year, as is common in other English language programs.

The client could choose from among three basic programs: Personal English Training, basically a one-on-one tutorial; Executive English Training, offered only in the summer and providing groups of five to ten students with business lectures in the morning and language training in the afternoon; and Special English Training, programs designed to meet special client needs – for example, programs combining corporate language training with other language, cultural, or management instruction offered by the institution. The programs usually had twenty-five hours of in-class instruction per week. In addition, they would provide access to social and business contacts outside of class hours. At the time I became involved as director, the materials generated by these outside contacts had little structured relationship to the in-class work unless individual instructors were particularly skilled in integrating them. A conversation partners component provided weekly opportunities for students to practice language in a social context.

Much of the raw material for an effective curriculum was there. What was lacking was an organizing principle to provide clarity, coherence, consistency, and continuity to the programs. Much later these four words came jokingly to being called "the four *C*'s" by the people involved in the curriculum development process. In any case, it was this lack that sent me looking for an organizing principle and for a way of implementing the principle to meet our program needs.

Research

One of my first tasks was to find out as much as possible about the history and delivery of the programs at the two sites used by the institution. Because this research had to be sandwiched between the immediate work on hand, it took several months. Summer was upon us, traditionally the busiest season for these kinds of programs, because businesspeople often take vacations or leaves of absence during this time to work on their English language skills. By mid-July, there were nine programs running simultaneously, occupying eleven instructors. These programs were one-on-one tutorials of two, three, four, or five weeks' duration. Two of the programs were split tutorials, with two instructors working together, usually one in the morning and the second in the afternoon. It was also expected that our largest client would send us between six and eight students in mid-September for a twenty-week program. In addition, our division had mandated that corporate language programs expand course offerings through aggressive marketing during the coming year. The assumption was that there would be a substantial increase in students in the next fiscal year. This heavy teaching workload coupled with the intense business side of the program delivery during the summer and early fall gave us even more data to analyze as we sorted out what might be the best type of curriculum. All of the instructors contributed ideas and suggestions on how to plan and implement the many different kinds of programs offered during this period.

In these first weeks of looking into the history of the development of the corporate language programs, I found that the pedagogical philosophy of the institution informed this language-learning program, just as it does all the learning programs the institution provides. The mission of the institution directs that all learning be based on a strong experiential component, and this approach was an important part of the marketing literature to clients. For example, there was emphasis on language practice in the local business community, and clients were assured that the context of the learning was business-related to reflect their needs. What was not in place was a clear definition of how the in-class work was to be experiential. Thus there was some confusion for clients during the negotiation process and for students upon arrival. It seemed an important part of the curriculum design that a clear explanation of this philosophy be communicated to clients and students before the programs began and be clarified if necessary during program delivery.

While searching out guidelines for program delivery, I discovered that some effective curriculum development work had been done for one of the Special English Training programs at the institution's second site. Although certain elements of that curriculum were being adapted to Personal English Training at that site, there was little consistency in program delivery among the programs and virtually none between the two sites. Much "reinventing of the wheel" was commonplace.

In addition, I conducted a very informal survey of client needs and of our competition in the field of executive English training. The client survey was basically a reading of the files of all the programs that had been run for the previous two years, checking the initial letters of inquiry and other correspondence for client expectations. I was able to see that client needs were becoming more diverse. The survey of the competition consisted of talking at length to those who were marketing our programs and to colleagues in other areas of the country involved with similar programs and looking for literature about these kinds of programs in professional journals. There wasn't much; it was apparent that we needed more hard information about competitors, and in the fall our departmental director initiated a marketing research project. Those results showed that this was becoming an increasingly competitive field.

Another professional research activity influenced our curriculum design process. In addition to my work with the corporate language programs, I was finishing my master's thesis, which was on the topic of self-evaluation and self-motivation for learners. The thesis was based on a model for facilitating independent and autonomous learning that I had been teaching in the two years since doing my course work for my master's degree. My involvement with this project had brought me in contact with much of the literature being published on the concept of learning to learn, or learner training, including *Learning to Learn English* by Gail Ellis and Barbara Sinclair (1990); *Teaching How to Learn* by Ken Willing (1989), part of a research series published by the National Centre for English Language Teaching and Research at Macquarie University in Australia; and *Self-instruction in Language Learning* by Leslie Dickinson (1987). Other reading helped clarify and inform my thinking at this time, for example, *Implementing the Learner-centred Curriculum,* edited by Jill Burton (1987); *Techniques and Principles in Language Teaching* by Diane Larsen-Freeman (1986); and *English for Specific Purposes: A Learning-centered Approach* by Tom Hutchinson and Alan Waters (1987).

As I worked with instructors and students over the summer, that reading reinforced my growing conviction that the focus for the programs being offered to corporate clients needed to shift from the narrow goal of mastering specific skills during the period of campus study to teaching the learners to perceive language learning as an ongoing process that is within their control. Instead of seeing the mastery of specific language skills as the only product that we were marketing, we needed to change our outlook and to market a process as well – the process of enabling students to acquire the skills to study the language independently. Thus we would be providing our clients with skilled learners capable of continued learning in their workplace.

Listening

During those busy days coordinating the programs' delivery, I began to hear recurring comments from instructors and students reflecting dissatisfaction and frustration with the existing system. The instructors and I met every Friday afternoon to share what was and wasn't working and brainstorm possible solutions to the challenges of delivering language-learning programs when almost all of us were new to the institution and many were new to teaching in a corporate environment. I also met with all the students each Friday for a feedback session, in which we focused on the students' living and learning environments. Most of the students were remarkably open in sharing both their doubts and sense of discouragement and their pleasures and sense of accomplishment. Other information about the students' thoughts and feelings came from the instructors' feedback sessions.

For the most part, the instructors' mentioned a high level of frustration with a system that made exceptional demands on their professional resources while providing little support for their efforts. Many of the students' comments on the learning environment reflected panic that the progress they were making in their study of the language would be lost upon their return to their work, whether in the United States or overseas. I began to review the system from the standpoints of both the instructors' and the students' needs.

I also received feedback from the clients, both through my initial contacts with them in establishing the programs and from their responses to the end-of-program progress reports. In some instances, the client and the student were one and the same, for corporate executives would often initiate programs of study independent of their employer's sponsorship. In these cases, the accountability was to the client-student, and I was able to get the information I needed from the weekly feedback sessions and the end-of-program evaluations. In other cases, students were sent by corporations, and our accountability was to both client and student. Information from the client about the success of our programs came through telephone conversations, letters, our reporting system, and their continued business.

My institution was very interested in and supportive of the development of the corporate language programs. During this time, I had weekly meetings with the director of programs, and the departmental director and the division director frequently asked for updates and made an effort to provide information and support when asked. They shared their vision of how the corporate language programs fit in with the other offerings of the Department of Language Services.

Experience

Further material for this review process came as I began to team-teach a group of four students in the twenty-week program that began in mid-September. The other instructor and I both had strong feelings about the lack of curriculum guidelines available. How could we bring the clarity, coherence, consistency, and continuity, which we had earlier identified as essential, to our work and to the corporate language programs? That dialogue and similar conversations with colleagues at both sites had considerable impact on the curriculum development process. In addition, our experiences with student learning over the next four months gave me much to work with in my search for a structure – a curriculum framework – for the many types of programs being offered. As it turned out, the development of the curriculum grew naturally from my listening to feedback from the instructors, students, and clients; from my experience teaching in the program, from my research work in the field of self-directed learning; and from the marketing research and the institutional mandates resulting from that research.

Development

The development of the curriculum framework was a long-term process occurring over a period of many months. The key elements of that curriculum framework gradually revealed themselves as I taught in and coped with directing the corporate language programs. The questions that seemed to demand answers were these:

1. What could we reasonably expect to accomplish in on-site language training programs of one to twenty weeks duration?
2. What curriculum framework would be adaptable to programs of such varying lengths for individuals with diverse cultural, business, and personal backgrounds, learning styles, and language proficiencies?
3. How could a curriculum framework provide consistency and continuity and still leave room for the individual experience, creativity, and initiative of instructors – one of our perceived strengths?

4. What kind of curriculum framework would be most useful for instructors and allow them to be ready to provide a language- and cultural-training program within a day or two of a student's arrival, often with little advance notice or prearrival information?

For me, the first of these questions became the crucial one. It was obvious that we were not going to be able to provide what the clients and the students thought we should, that is, that the students would, in whatever period of time they had for study, leave their programs fluent in English. No matter how much we worked with students in defining specific goals and objectives for their programs, the students seemed to feel that an intensive immersion program would work miracles in all skill areas, and they would walk away masters of the language. They may not have been fully conscious of this expectation, but as we monitored responses to the training over the course of their programs, we could almost count on a panic reaction near the end of the course of study, a kind of "What's wrong with me, you, or the program that I am not speaking English like a native speaker?" Reflection on this phenomenon produced some careful analysis of the goal- and objective-writing process. We revised our approach and began to focus our work with our clients and students on producing goals and objectives that were specific, measurable, and achievable. Two books that were helpful at this juncture were *Assessing Achievement in the Learner-Centred Curriculum* by Geoff Brindley (1989) and *Learner English: A Teacher's Guide to Interference and Other Problems* edited by Michael Swan and Bernard Smith (1987).

This work on the student's goal- and objective-writing process forced us to think of ways of educating clients to accept the kind of language-learning programs that best met the needs they communicated to us. The challenge was to move the client from a focus on results expressed solely in terms of a product (mastery of specific skills, such as pronunciation) to focus on results that are also based on the perception of learning as a process. In other words, we were trying to educate our clients to the concept of language study as a long-term, ongoing learning process that can be self-directed by the learner. We needed to convince and assure clients that this process could eventually result in mastery of the language, to whatever standard desired. Thus what we offered was a process contributing to a product – learning that results in mastery.

We were further challenged to find ways of communicating our approach in terms that our corporate clients could understand and value. These terms are often very different from the academic terminology that we as educators are accustomed to using. Different nomenclature helped. Students became *participants* or *trainees;* teachers became *instructors* or *trainers;* courses became *training programs.* As the curriculum framework evolved, so did a terminology couched in a business context that made that framework and its underlying philosophy more accessible to our clients.

It was out of the work with goals and objectives that the broader aspects of the first question began to tease my imagination. If a student had only two or three weeks to work on language learning, what expectations were reasonable for that learning? Obviously, not much was going to be accomplished in pronunciation work. Significantly altering sound production in adults who have been speaking very little English or speaking English in a certain way for many years was too much to expect. In the same way, mastering the complexities of all English verb tenses, if the current level of mastery was the present tense with occasional use of the simple past, was unrealistic. Raising listening comprehension levels was a bit easier to accomplish with concentrated practice on this skill, but there were limits to the improvement possible in a given time frame (Ur 1984.) So what could we do?

It seemed to me that the first thing we could reasonably do was help students become aware of their language-learning needs. The process would require obtaining as much information as possible about the corporation's expectations for a particular student. We also felt we could benefit by knowing something of the students' levels of proficiency – if possible, before arrival. The awareness of individual learning needs we wished to foster would need to encompass the linguistic, functional, and cultural learning needs of the student, and we asked that proficiency be assessed in these three areas. This need had been recognized for some time at the other site, and some work had been done in developing instruments to elicit this information from clients. We began to develop better instruments, choosing to get this information by using detailed but "user-friendly" questionnaires in the form of checklists, as they would be answered by busy people who perhaps had little knowledge themselves of a language-learning needs assessment process.

If appropriate, we asked the immediate supervisor of the student or the corporate liaison person to answer a series of questions about the student's need for English in the workplace and to assess the student's current level of proficiency. In addition, some clients provided the results of proficiency tests, such as the TOEIC or the TOEFL, that had been administered prior to the student's arrival. We also needed, before arrival, as much information as possible of students' perceptions of their learning needs. Thus we also asked students to fill out needs assessment questionnaires (see Appendix B) and to send samples of any work they were currently doing in English or might later be doing. These samples were used in our program planning.

Developing appropriate methods for evaluating proficiency in the three areas and determining which methods worked best for specific programs became an important element in designing what was to become the first component of the curriculum framework. We eventually adopted the SPEAK test as a pre- and posttest for all programs. For longer programs, we used the TOEIC test as a needs assessment tool, and for very long programs it was used as a posttest. The search for the perfect evaluation method or methods for a diverse constituency continues to be a challenge.

Often we did not receive information prior to the student's arrival on campus, so the instructor and the student had to do a needs assessment on-site before a program plan could be finalized. During this process, instructors and students attempted to establish clearly the students' learning needs. It would be the instructor's responsibility, with the assistance of the director, to sort out any confusion in the mix of expectations among the four participants in this learning process – the student, the instructor, the client, and the institution delivering the service.

With or without advance information, the question of individual learning styles and students' awareness or lack of awareness of their own style was critical to that first question of what could reasonably be accomplished in an on-site program. It seemed important to help students gain insight as to their preferred learning style and to analyze that style's effectiveness in our learning environment. Most instructors faced student learning styles that produced initial resistance to the experiential learning philosophy of the institution and to the loosely organized program offerings we were presently providing. Struggling with this resistance wasted valuable learning time, especially in the shorter programs. It seemed a more efficient use of time to focus the learner's attention on this issue at the outset of a program and address any problem areas openly. This meant asking learners to look at their own learning and to assume control over how they were going to function in a particular learning environment. Out of that analysis of learning styles could come recommendations for modifying a learning style, if the instructor thought such modifications necessary. Some of us had already been doing this intuitively in our teaching; others found the concept intriguing but somewhat daunting. I began to explore ways in which this concept could be worked into all the programs we offered, no matter what their length. This idea raised issues of teacher training, as well as additional questions about learner training, already under consideration and study.

Most of the development of the concept of learner training that appears in the curriculum framework occurred during the twenty-week tutorial that I cotaught with a colleague. It was an evolution of thought that grew out of listening to the students, listening to the corporate client's feedback to the biweekly reports we filed, and listening to our own perceptions of what was working effectively and what needed our attention and creativity.

That evolution can clearly be traced by looking at one of the first learning activities that I instituted in my program plan and then made a core element of all the programs we offered. This was called the "outside learning activity," a structured weekly activity that asked students to move out into the community to fulfill an assigned task. The activity had a linguistic, a functional, and a cultural objective and a structured follow-up. One example of such an activity was attendance at the local Rotary Club meeting. The four students were given information about the organization — purpose, members, scheduled program that week. They chose the linguistic objective individually, depending on their particular need, and the functional and cultural objectives were established with the instructor's help. The follow-up activity was designed to give practice in particular skills they needed. These students had requested presentation skills practice and so were assigned to give five-minute presentations about some aspect of the Rotary Club meeting that they had chosen beforehand. These presentations were videotaped, and the tape was used in many follow-up exercises, from linguistic error analysis and correction to presentation skills practice.

In the process of designing weekly activities for all the programs then running, the instructors and I became aware that the exposure to the community was resulting in a great deal of rich material for in-class work. We also became aware that what we didn't work on in class, the students were finding ways of working on outside of class. They were often asking for our help with this outside work. Furthermore, responding to individual requests for assistance with out-of-class learning also kept us more informed about and responsive to individual learning needs in class. When I received a request from our students asking that their individual learning needs somehow be addressed in the class, we subsequently designed self-study independent learning activities for thirty-minute periods of in-class time three times a week as a means of providing learning opportunities for the other students while we worked with individual students.

This shift in the design of the program I was working in, my continued work on my thesis, and an experience with deciding what aspects of our teaching or training that the instructors wished to work on in our Professional Development Program brought the concept of self-study independent learning to the forefront of my thinking. This Professional Development Program was a structured outgrowth of our summer instructors' meetings. In two-hour sessions each Friday afternoon, instructors in the corporate language programs and the International Student of English Program met voluntarily to discuss issues and concerns about effective ESL learning. The topic of self-study for learners was one such issue on our agenda.

Another experience influenced my thinking about reasons for self-study and ways and means of providing opportunities for it. The students in the twenty-week program were to have a two-week homestay over the holidays. In preparing them for this experience, I began to look at what strategies they could use to continue to work on their language during this time.

For one week prior to their leaving for their various host families, I asked them to focus their attention on what strategies they thought they might use to continue to work on their language over the two-week homestay period. We worked out what I called a self-study plan.

Each student identified a specific goal for language study for the two weeks, and then we brainstormed possible ways of achieving that goal. One of the students wanted to work intensively on building vocabulary during the homestay. He designed a method for using a vocabulary journal that would enable him to record new vocabulary, work out ways to use it, and then record his experiences with its use. Another student identified pronunciation as a goal. She worked out a way of adapting the sound production method we had been using in class to her needs for the homestay. She also chose to work in a journal to record progress with her self-study plan. The other students made similar plans and also used journals as a means of recording progress.

A final example of an experience that influenced the design of the curriculum framework occurred in the final four weeks of the twenty-week program. One of the recurrent plaints heard from client and student alike was, "What is going to happen to my language when I return to work?" Clients were asking us what could be done at the job site to encourage continued study and use of the language. Students were asking us for ideas for continued study. In response to these concerns and requests from our current group, we decided to look closely at what was possible in preparing them to continue the language-learning process independently on their return to their countries and to their workplace. We also had the unique perspective of a new instructor who happened to be skilled at looking at reentry issues.

The four students were not going directly back to Japan. They were going to their U.S. corporate headquarters for varying lengths of time for on-the-job training. We had a visit from their U.S. corporate training coordinator during the posthomestay debriefing, in which we looked at the efficacy of the homestay self-study learning plans the students had designed. In that process, we analyzed progress (or lack of progress) toward their goals and the reasons for it. The training coordinator made a presentation of what they could expect as to living environments and learning environments when they arrived at the headquarters. It was apparent from the students' questions that great anxiety surrounded this coming experience, and much of this anxiety centered around their language proficiency.

We had already decided to expand the self-study learning plan of the homestay to their return to Japan. We decided to provide an interim step in the process by having them first set goals and objectives for language learning during the on-the-job training and then set goals and objectives for continued self-study of the language on their return home. We used materials from a wide variety of sources designed to enable the students to reassess their preferred learning styles and their current levels of linguistic, functional, and cultural proficiency, to analyze the amount of time they would have available for self-study, to define the uses for which they would need English in their work environment, and to establish goals and objectives for continued self-study. Although the implementation of this collaborative process for the design of an independent ongoing learning plan was somewhat rough the first time, we learned from the experience and worked on refining our skills in facilitating the process. It was the design of this last activity, an independent on-going learning plan, that brought together all the pieces of research, listening, and experience that I had been accruing over the past months. That coming together and a casual conversation with a colleague produced the concept for the subject of this chapter, a curriculum framework.

Curriculum framework

The concept that emerged expressed itself in terms of a training goal. It seemed that we could best serve our clients and our students if we could provide training that would enable learners, with the assistance of their instructors (1) to assess their learning needs; analyze their learning styles; define learning objectives that were specific, measurable, and achievable within a given time; and participate in planning a program that would meet those objectives; (2) to implement that program plan through the practice of carefully selected learning strategies to achieve those objectives; and (3) to design a self-study plan to continue their learning after their on-site work with us. This concept for learning, with its three key elements, also had the advantage of conforming to the mission of our institution, which is dedicated to serving the whole individual and to empowering people to be independent and in control of their own lives and their own learning.

As I continued to mull over this concept for learning, I began to see the three key elements as a framework within which we could provide for individual program design in which the student is fully invested in the process, provide consistency and continuity within and among programs, and foster instructor creativity and initiative in all phases of the curriculum. The word *framework* seemed appropriate because, given the parameters of the corporate language programs currently being marketed by this institution, we needed to provide for flexibility and responsiveness to client and student needs. Because we were going to continue to provide personalized programs on demand, we would have large numbers of adjunct faculty doing single tutorials or split tutorials in Personal English Training or working as training teams in Special English Training for various lengths of time. It also seemed important to define the curriculum in terms that would provide support and guidance for instructors without stifling their initiative and creativity. The concept of a framework gave instructors a structure for this process. The feedback I received from colleagues reinforced my conviction that such a term was appropriate and the concept it represented was needed.

I began now to look at the third question: What should be included in a framework to help instructors and students take maximum advantage of the time in which they had to work? Planning is crucial to the success of any training program. Instructors who had the kind of planning skills that enabled them to respond quickly and effectively to the needs assessment process were the ones, for example, who were able to move calmly through the challenge of a two-week tutorial with little advance notice. In my own planning process, I had developed a three-step approach that I found to be particularly effective in the delivery of corporate training programs.

This approach was based in part on student feedback on what they felt they needed to be more comfortable in their new learning environment. Most of these individuals were older adults who had been away from a study environment for a fair amount of time. Some had the conviction that their age was going to be a barrier to their learning. Others found the return to a learning environment somewhat threatening. After being in positions of authority over others, it was sometimes difficult to see themselves having a teacher in authority over them. Some found the whole aspect of being vulnerable extremely difficult. They did not want to appear foolish or childish, as they often felt they were when they could not express themselves fluently in English. Another barrier was the learning philosophy of our institution, which often demanded that the students be willing to take risks and make mistakes from which they could learn, to be flexible and open to a variety of learning styles.

I had found that it was very important to hear what these corporate executives felt they needed to know about their programs. These businesspeople were used to working with clearly defined objectives and time frames. Most of them had daily diaries in which they planned their days' work. They expected to have a plan of their program and a schedule of what was going to happen and when. If these elements were missing, they became extremely uncomfortable, and their adjustment to the learning environment was made more difficult. It was thus important to meet these businesspeople halfway, as it were, and to provide for the communication of their program design in ways that they could understand and were used to.

The curriculum framework began to shape itself into three components to be applied to all programs: (1) designing the program learning plan, (2) implementing the program learning plan, and (3) setting up the independent on-going learning plan (see Appendix A).

Designing the program learning plan

As the first component of the curriculum framework began to assume its shape, we decided that a program learning plan should be written, to include the following elements, communicated to the student in a form acceptable to the program director, the instructor, the student, and, if appropriate, the client:

1. Needs assessment, including the administration of formal instruments of assessment common to all programs, the use of informal assessment tools by individual instructors, and the determination of the degree of need for learner training to foster the independence and autonomy of the student in the program
2. Learning styles analysis
3. Specific, measurable, and achievable goals and objectives
4. Specification of learning strategies that would best enable the learner to achieve those goals and objectives, using the awareness of the student and the expertise of the instructor
5. Community contacts and conversation partners, if applicable,
6. Opportunities for independent self-study outside of class
7. Weekly schedule for learning, in and out of class

Implementing the program learning plan

The design of the second component of the curriculum framework involved analyzing the elements we had been including in corporate tutorials and deciding which ones we felt were core elements and which were what came to be termed variable elements. The core elements would be included in all offered programs. The variable elements would be available for instructors to work into program design for specific student needs.

We searched for commonalities among all the programs we had offered over the past year. Out of that search, we came up with several core elements (see Appendix A). Two of these elements reflect skills to be worked on. However, the majority of the elements are designed to provide learner training in using learning strategies effectively and in independent self-study techniques. These eight elements now define the basic program we offer to all clients and students.

We then turned our attention to the variable elements. Again, we analyzed past programs for commonly requested elements. The list was longer than the core elements with the potential for being expanded or modified as the needs of the world's business communities change. This list contains primarily skill-based elements. For example, if a student arrives needing to work on presentation skills, the instructor includes that variable element in the program learning plan. Another student may need to work on reading reports quickly for the main idea. The instructor can go to the curriculum resource file and draw on the reading methods available for this variable element and easily incorporate it into the program learning plan.

The primary advantage of working with a framework for curriculum design is that such a format is adaptable to changes that occur in the marketplace. Defining curriculum content by core and variable elements enables everyone using the framework to tailor programs to meet individual needs, be they for single tutorials in a corporate setting or for courses in a more academic learning environment.

Setting up the independent ongoing learning plan

The third and final component of the curriculum framework to be designed was the independent ongoing learning plan. Drawing on our experience with the twenty-week program, I looked at the elements that constituted the process of ongoing independent learning. It seemed to me that it was a reflection of what we had determined to be the focus for learning in the program learning plan. In other words, an independent ongoing learning plan would be designed by analyzing the language learner's needs, desig- nating specific learning strategies to enable the learner to meet those needs, defining a time frame within which the learner could continue to progress in the study of the language, and assembling the tools and resources that will help in the process. All of this would take place before the student left the program.

In conversation with yet another talented colleague, we questioned the effectiveness of the independent ongoing learning plan when an individual is back in the myriad work and social relationships in which the student's first language is the primary means of communication. To be supportive of such a learning plan, we found it necessary to build some means of follow- on into the curriculum framework. Our experience is showing us that such a system is indeed needed. We have several ideas of how this might be accomplished.

The first month seems crucial, so we are establishing several means of communicating with former trainees and their supervisors. One idea is to have a telephone service in which for a limited period each week, the trainee calls an instructor who listens to reports on the effectiveness or problem areas of the learning plans and then makes constructive responses. Another idea is to send students away with preaddressed postcards on which they can report progress with their plans. A third possibility is to send a questionnaire to students soliciting their responses to questions carefully designed to inform us of the effectiveness of the plans being implemented. This questionnaire would be used primarily to examine and refine the learning plan process to make it more effective.

Further discussions with other colleagues resulted in a second important method for follow-on. We will send an instructor to the student's country to conduct a six-month workshop on learning plan maintenance. Corporations who have sent several students to the program have proved receptive to this idea. Such a workshop is also good feedback for evaluating the effectiveness of our curriculum framework, for keeping up with the changes in the marketplace, and tracking the continued progress of our students.

Implementing the curriculum modifications

As we teach this curriculum framework, we are learning much about its strengths and also about its problem areas. It does seem to be truly adaptable to almost any program. The one exception so far was a one-week tutorial with a specific skill focus in which there just wasn't enough time to work on the concept of independent ongoing learning. Possibly, students who are very advanced in their language proficiency may arrive with such specific skill needs and such a limited time frame that our learner training and self-study concept may be inappropriate.

Other modifications continue to occur. We are continually finding creative ways to evaluate progress in corporate programs. Corporations are used to seeing progress reported in quantifiable terms, whereas ESL instructors are used to couching progress in qualitative terms. As we work with the curriculum framework, we are finding that the independent self-study learning strategies can be designed with evaluation criteria that are quantifiable in ways that instructors can be comfortable with.

One very effective addition to the curriculum framework has been the incorporation of more practice opportunities with self-study learning strategies. This was in response to the amount of time it was taking to get students invested in the concept of themselves as ongoing language learners and to increase their knowledge of these strategies. Instructors now working in the program have designed optional structured exercises using learning strategies in the four basic skill areas to be done outside of class. The students receive a checklist each week, in addition to the weekly schedule, in which their in-class work is listed as well as the optional learning strategy exercises. Students hand in these checklists at the end of the week, and instructors have a good sense of who is showing the kind of initiative necessary to become an ongoing language learner.

Conclusion

The curriculum framework enabled a loose collection of individual programs to achieve consistency through a clearly defined course of corporate language programs with the kind of *clarity* and *continuity* that would work effectively with unpredictable client and participant schedules, with frequent turnover in instructor personnel, and with the diverse individual needs of the students. Having a curriculum framework that was the same for all programs, a menu of learning strategies from which individual instructors could pick and choose, and a learner-centered focus that promoted independent and ongoing learning gave the corporate language programs the *coherence* that had been lacking. The three curriculum components and their supporting core and variable elements gave instructors a framework within which they received support in a challenging and demanding learning environment and in which they were free to use all the *creativity* at their command. The four C's became, in the end, five – all of which were essential to this approach to effective language training.

Reviewing the curriculum design process

As I conclude this description of one curriculum design process, I ask myself what the primary challenge in the design of the curriculum and in the teaching of it was and what I would have done differently. The primary challenge has been to educate clients and students to accept the concept of language study as a long-term ongoing process that can be most effective when self-directed by the learner. In other words, the challenge was to move both client and student from a perception of learning as a result expressed solely in terms of a product toward a perception of learning as an ongoing process.

There isn't much in the broad scope of the process I have described that I would change. The design of this curriculum was based on careful listening to the four parties involved in corporate language learning: the students, the instructors implementing the programs, the corporate clients, and the institution delivering the service. Out of that listening came an assessment of the needs that a curriculum would have to address. Also out of that listening came a sense of how the curriculum must be structured to support the student, the instructor, the client, and the institution. This seems to me the most effective way of designing a curriculum that will be responsive to the people it is to serve.

I am also convinced that structural flexibility is essential to curriculum design. Once the program standards criteria have been established, it is important to implement those criteria in a way that allows for creativity and initiative while providing for quality control. Too often we are presented with a curriculum so prescriptive in its structure that we build failure into its implementation. Who has not been presented with a curriculum that demands that so many verb tenses, some modals, comparative and superlative adjectives, count and noncount nouns, and a number of other linguistic elements all be covered in a period of a few weeks? If that curriculum is very enlightened, we may also be asked to look at appropriate functional language issues and address the cross-cultural needs of the learners.

On the one hand, in such an example, if we listen to our learners and go with what they need and can truly accommodate in the time we have with them, we usually end up scrapping any number of the prescribed curriculum elements. We then feel like failures in the eyes of the institution and perhaps our colleagues and ourselves. The choice on the other hand is even worse, in my opinion. We decide to implement what the curriculum demands, we cram the learning into heads that are swimming with overload, and we fail again, but in a different way: This time we fail the learners, who may retain little of such learning. I have also had the experience of being handed curriculum guidelines that are so broadly stated that they offer little support or guidance. These usually leave me feeling insecure as to how the standards of the institution are enforced and frustrated over the amount of preparation I must do unassisted.

With a framework such as the one described here, I feel we have the best of all possible worlds: enough structure to provide quality control and consistency in program delivery for the institution, support for the people responsible for delivering the programs, room for creativity and initiative in that delivery, and flexibility to meet the changing needs of the client base.

Appendix A: Curriculum framework

Curriculum Framework

COMPONENTS

I. Designing the program learning plan
II. Implementing the program learning plan
III. Setting up the independent ongoing learning plan

I. Designing the program learning plan

SCHEMA OF DESIGN PROCESS

Student
(brings needs)   **Corporation**
                                                        (sends expectations)

Instructor
(uses professional language-learning expertise)

Synthesis
(of all factors)

Program Learning Plan

   A. Needs assessment
      1. Formal
      2. Informal
      3. Learner training needs
   B. Learning styles analysis
   C. Goals and objectives
      1. Specific
      2. Measurable
      3. Achievable
   D. Learning strategies to achieve goals and objectives
   E. Community contacts, conversation partner
   F. Independent study outside of class
   G. Schedule
II. Implementing the program learning plan
   A. Core curriculum elements
      1. Structured pronunciation practice
      2. Listening comprehension practice
      3. Error analysis and correction strategies

   4. Weekly outside learning activity

   5. Independent ongoing learning strategies

   6. Community contacts and conversation partners

   7. Weekly feedback session with program administrator

   8. Report writing: accountability to the client

  B. Variable curriculum elements

   1. Computer composition: business memos, reports, letters

   2. Reading comprehension and fluency

   3. Dialogue journal writing

   4. Specific crosscultural or multicultural awareness training

   5. Learning strategies through case studies

   6. Functional language for business and social contexts

   7. Vocabulary practice

   8. Idiomatic language practice

   9. Focused grammar practice

   10. Presentation skills

   11. Business meeting skills

   12. Negotiation, persuasion, clarification

   13. Other business skills

III. Setting up the independent ongoing learning plan

  A. Before departure

   1. Analyze ongoing learning needs

   2. Determine appropriate learning strategies

   3. Define time frame for language study

   4. Assemble tools and resources

  B. Back at work

   1. Initial follow-on

   2. Three-month questionnaire

   3. Six-month follow-on workshop in student's country

Appendix B: Sample needs assessment

Corporate Language Programs Needs Assessment

Your answers to the following questions will provide needed information for planning an effective and efficient individualized language training program. Please answer the questions as fully as possible. When there are choices, circle the best one.

1. My English should be good enough to: (Choose the five most important: 1 = most important, 2 = second most important, etc.)

_____ introduce myself	_____ introduce others	_____ make a good impression
_____ engage in small talk	_____ instruct others	_____ persuade others
_____ give presentations	_____ understand presentations	_____ speak at meetings
_____ plan projects	_____ discuss things one to one	_____ speak on the phone
_____ write letters	_____ write telexes or faxes	_____ make appointments

_____ understand discussions at formal meetings   _____ write reports or summaries

_____ participate in large group discussions   _____ play a role in negotiations

_____ present or discuss offers   _____ show people around places

_____ take notes at meetings or conferences   _____ listen to and understand speeches and lectures

_____ read reports and correspondence   _____ read newspapers and magazines

_____ read instruction manuals or technical journals

2. The most important use of my English in the near future will be _____
3. The full name of my company is _____
4. I have worked at my company for _____ months/years.
5. My company specializes in _____
6. Its headquarters are in _____
7. It owns subsidiaries in _____ (how many) countries. These include _____
8. It employs _____ (how many) people.
9. The place I work is _____ (where). The division I work in is _____
10. I am responsible for _____

11. I am responsible to _____.
    (name and position)
12. My department consists of _____.
    (number of employees and positions)
13. I deal mainly with _____ (persons).
14. My tasks are to _____
15. Please circle the words that are closest to your feeling about your job and your need for English:

    My job is: interesting   For my career, English is: useful
                boring
                challenging   necessary
                routine
                time-consuming   vital
                rewarding

16. The last English course I attended was _____,
    and I completed this in _____
17. English-speaking countries I have visited include _____
18. This is my _____ (number) time in the United States.
19. In my own language, I speak: frequently/very little
                                   quickly/slowly
20. I enjoy talking about (list things you like to talk about business, politics, sports, people, music, travel, etc.) _____
21. I know a lot about _____
22. I could give a talk on _____
23. I have given talks on _____ to _____
24. I need English to talk to (list all persons: boss, clients, customers, colleagues, suppliers, trainees, agents, staff, members, etc.)

    _____

25. The most important people I will be speaking to in English are

    _____

(Adapted from Pauleen 1990)

ANALYSIS AND TASKS

Laura Hull entered the course design process in a way familiar to many teachers: She was asked to teach a course with little time to prepare and few guidelines. However, the chapter is not about that particular course but about how she developed a curriculum framework for planning and implementing such courses, individualized courses for a diverse clientele of business executives. The frustration of the initial experience clearly indicated that there was a need for such a framework so that the program would not cause teachers continually to "reinvent the wheel." The development of the framework encompassed three phases: defining the challenges, figuring out how to meet the challenges, and formalizing the solution.

In the first phase, Hull gathered information that helped her problematize the situation – to understand and define the challenges so that she could make the changes needed. She researched how the programs had developed and how they were marketed to prospective client companies. She researched what clients had contracted for – their needs – and how they evaluated the programs. She sought input from teachers and students who were currently involved in the program: What did they perceive as the strengths and problems of their courses and of the program? Her own team teaching in a twenty-week course was both a context for making sense of the research and another source of ideas about what was needed and what could be done. Finally, in addition to gathering information, she was also influenced by her research on learner training, or how to help learners develop their learning skills and strategies.

This first phase, understanding and defining the challenges, can also be viewed as a process of formative evaluation, evaluation done during the development or implementation of a program for purposes of improving it. Hull's experience underscores the ongoing and contingent role that evaluation plays in course development: She was evaluating an existing program that she was both adminstering and teaching in. The evaluation took many forms. It included weekly feedback meetings with students and teachers about what was working and what wasn't, reading client files to determine what their expectations of the program were, reviewing course evaluations by clients and students to see whether their expectations were being fulfilled, reviewing existing curriculum documents, and conversations with her coteacher. The teaching and research helped her problematize the situation in terms of questions that needed to be addressed in the curriculum: how to set realistic objectives for each course, how to adapt to a variety of needs and program lengths, and how to implement courses without a lot of teacher preparation and yet support teachers' initiative and creativity. The questions in turn led to the second phase, finding workable answers.

Answering the questions required a close look at the differing expectations of the companies, the students, the instructors, and the institution. One problem that soon became apparent was the conflict between the institution's educational philosophy as implemented in the classes and the students' expectations of how they would be taught. There was also a mismatch between the clients' expectations and what the instructors felt could be done within the time frame of a given course. Another problem was the instructors' feeling that they received little support from the institution. The students also expressed concerns about holding on to what they had learned once they left the classroom.

Reconciling the various expectations and needs was a central purpose in the development of the curriculum. It involved determining what was feasible within the constraints of each course and developing the ability to set realistic objectives for each student or group of students. Hull came to the conclusion that the one achievable goal for any program, regardless of length, was to help students devise a learning plan that they could undertake in the classroom and then continue after the program was over. Designing such a plan required the development of needs assessment tools, on the one hand, and, on the other, finding ways to communicate to the students and their companies what results could realistically be achieved in the program.

Needs assessment involved testing for proficiency to determine the students' level of English competency, seeking information about how the students used or were expected to use English, and finding out how the students perceived their own needs. Ideally, this was to be done prior to the student's arrival, but more often than not it had to be done on-site, as part of the course.

Hull's own experience with and commitment to learner training played a central role in the development of the curriculum. In Hull's conceptualization, learner training included both understanding learning styles and learning to direct one's own learning. Understanding learning styles meant that learners became aware of their preferred ways of learning, analyzed their benefits and drawbacks, and learned new ways as necessary. Learning to direct one's own learning entailed devising goals and deciding on strategies for fulfilling them in each learning situation. Hull gives two examples of the latter, one called the outside learning activity, which students undertake in conjunction with their classes, and the other a plan for independent study during a two-week homestay with an American family. Both became an integral part of the curriculum, but they did not start out that way. Hull describes how the outside learning activity began as something productive for the other students in a class to do while the instructors worked one-on-one with a classmate. Hull makes the point that much of what became codified in the curriculum was as much the result of invention and necessity as the desire to put her beliefs into practice.

The third phase of the process was putting together the framework itself. The framework consisted of three steps: designing a learning plan, implementing the learning plan, and setting up an ongoing learning plan to be carried out once students had left the program. The framework had the advantage of being flexible but also giving the instructors guidelines and a sense of accountability. In devising the objectives, the instructors had a list of core elements and variable elements to draw on while designing the program learning plan. The curriculum framework is thus a process, not a product. It is not a specification of what should be taught but rather a guide for how to set up a program for each student that meets the criteria Hull articulated in phase 1: It helps set realistic objectives for each course, it can be adapted to a variety of needs and program lengths, it makes use of the initiative and creativity of the instructors, and it provides them with a set of guidelines that they can draw on, with little advance notice, to develop their course.

FOCUS ON EVALUATION

1. J. D. Brown (1989) gives the following definition of evaluation: "the systematic collection and analysis of all relevant information necessary to promote the improvement of a curriculum and assess its effectiveness and efficiency, as well as the participants' attitudes within the context of the particular institutions involved" (223).
   - How does this definition fit Hull's work? Give examples.
   - Which aspects of her work does it not fit? Why not?
2. Hutchinson and Waters (1987) make a distinction between learner assessment and course evaluation. Learner assessment includes testing students for purposes of placement, assessing proficiency, diagnosing gaps and needs, and assessing achievement.
   - Which kind of learner assessment does Hull include in her curriculum planning?
   - Which kinds of learner assessment will you include in your course?
   - What means will you use to carry out such assessment?
3. Formative evaluation is the process of evaluating any aspect of a course as it is being developed and implemented for the purposes of improving it.
   - What role will formative evaluation play in the development of your course?
   - Who will have input?
   - How and how often will you carry it out?

4. Summative evaluation is carried out once the course is over, or a stage of the course is over, for purposes of evaluating the effectiveness of the course, primarily in meeting its stated goals and objectives within the scope of the curriculum. The results of summative evaluation can determine whether a course should or should not be continued.
   - What form will summative evaluation take in your course?
   - Who will have access to this information, and for what purpose?
5. A key issue in Hull's course development was the need to find out the expectations of the various parties involved and then to find ways to reconcile them.
   - In your course, who are the parties, and what expectations do they bring?
   - How do you know what their expectations are?
   - Which expectations are likely to be sources of conflict?
   - How do you propose to resolve those conflicts?
6. Hull problematized her situation first as a set of needs – the four C's of clarity, coherence, consistency and continuity – and then as a set of questions. Review the questions, on page 181. Then write two to four questions that frame the central requirements your course will need to address.

References

Brindley, G. 1989. *Assessing Achievement in the Learner-Centred Curriculum.* Sydney, Australia: Macquarie University, National Centre for English Language Teaching and Research.

Brown, J. D. 1989. Language program evaluation: A synthesis of existing possibilities. In R. K. Johnson, ed., *The Second Language Curriculum,* pp. 222–243. Cambridge: Cambridge University Press.

Burton, J., ed. 1987. *Implementing the Learner-Centred Curriculum.* Sydney: Australia: National Curriculum Resource Centre, Adult Migrant Education Program.

Dickinson, L. 1987. *Self-instruction in Language Learning.* Cambridge, England: Cambridge University Press.

Ellis, G., and B. Sinclair. 1990. *Learning to Learn English: A Course in Learner Training.* Cambridge: Cambridge University Press.

Hutchinson, T., and A. Waters. 1987. *English for Specific Purposes: A Learning-Centered Approach.* Cambridge: Cambridge University Press.

Larsen-Freeman, D. 1986. *Techniques and Principles in Language Teaching.* Oxford: Oxford University Press.

Pauleen, D. J. 1990. Starting and Running a Business English and Cross-cultural Skills Program for the Corporate Client. Unpublished master's thesis, School for International Training, Brattleboro, VT.

Swan, M., and B. Smith, eds. 1987. *Learner English: A Teacher's Guide to Interference and Other Problems.* Cambridge: Cambridge University Press.

Ur, P. 1984. *Teaching Listening Comprehension.* Cambridge: Cambridge University Press.

Willing, K. 1989. *Teaching How to Learn.* Sydney, Australia: Macquarie University, National Centre for English Language Teaching and Research.

Further reading

Historical overview

Yalden, J. 1987. *Principles of Course Design for Language Teaching*. New York: Cambridge University Press.

> Parts 1, 2, and 3 of this book give a clear analysis of how the emergence of communicative competence as the focus of language teaching has changed the role of the teacher, especially in the area of course design.

Clark, J. L. 1987. *Curriculum Renewal in School Foreign Language Learning*. Oxford: Oxford University Press.

> The first part of this book examines the effects of different Western educational value systems on curriculum development and renewal in general as well as in specific relation to the teaching of foreign languages.

Overview of curriculum development processes

Johnson, R. K. 1989. A decision-making framework for the coherent language curriculum. In R. K. Johnson, ed. *The Second Language Curriculum*, pp. 1–23. Cambridge: Cambridge University Press.

> This chapter serves as both an introduction to the book and as an overview of the processes of a language curriculum and the roles and responsibilities of the people involved in them.

Richards, J. C. 1990. *The Language Teaching Matrix*. New York: Cambridge University Press.

> The first chapter, "Curriculum Development in Second Language Teaching," provides concise definitions and clear explanations of the curriculum development processes of needs analysis, goals and objectives, syllabus design, methodology, and testing and evaluation.

Needs assessment

Berwick, R. 1989. Needs assessment in language programming: From theory to practice. In R. K. Johnson, ed., *The Second Language Curriculum,* pp. 48–62. Cambridge: Cambridge University Press.

This chapter provides discussion and examples of how beliefs about learning, language, and learners affect the way needs analyses are planned and carried out.

Brindley, G. P. 1984. *Needs Analysis and Objective Setting in the Adult Migrant Education Program.* Sydney, Australia: Adult Migrant Education Program.

This book examines teachers' and learners' roles in needs analysis. It shows how students can look critically at their own learning needs and assess their progress in relation to those needs, including techniques and strategies.

Brindley, G. P. 1989. The role of needs analysis in adult ESL program design. In R. K. Johnson, ed. *The Second Language Curriculum,* pp. 63–78. Cambridge: Cambridge University Press.

This chapter provides a comparison of approaches to needs analysis, an elaboration of "objective" and "subjective" needs, and discussion of the roles of teachers and learners in negotiating what should be learned and how in a learner-centered system.

Hutchinson, T., and A. Waters. 1987. *English for Specific Purposes: A Learning-Centered Approach.* Cambridge: Cambridge University Press.

Chapter 6, "Needs Analysis" proposes the distinction between target needs and learning needs and suggests ways to assess both.

Nunan, D. 1988. *Syllabus Design.* Oxford: Oxford University Press.

Pages 13–24 discuss the types and purposes of needs analysis and provide examples.

Nunan, D. 1988. *The Learner-Centred Curriculum.* Cambridge: Cambridge University Press.

Chapter 4 "Pre-Course Planning Procedures," discusses the pros and cons of needs analysis , who should participate, and how, with examples from an ESL context.

Tarone, E., and G. Yule. 1989. *Focus on the Language Learner.* New York: Oxford University Press.

This book defines types and purposes of needs analyses, with an emphasis on determining what is used in the "real world." It provides explanations of techniques for gathering data on needs, including a range of case studies of needs analyses done by teachers in ESL contexts.

Determining goals and objectives

Mager, R. F. 1962. *Preparing Instructional Objectives.* Belmont, Calif.: Fearon Publishers.

This is an oft-cited classic with a clear rationale and practical examples of performance-based objectives.

Nunan, D. 1988. *Syllabus Design.* Oxford: Oxford University Press.

Pages 24–25 and 79–84, discuss different ways to state goals and the rationale for each.

Saphier, J., and R. Gower. 1987. *The Skillful Teacher.* Carlisle, Mass.: Research for Better Teaching.

Chapter 15 , "Objectives," describes the authors' taxonomy of objectives with examples drawn from secondary school classrooms.

Stern, H. H. 1992. *Issues and Options in Language Teaching.* Oxford: Oxford University Press.

Part 2 "Defining Objectives," elaborates various taxonomies of educational objectives and their relationship to language learning.

Conceptualizing content
Communicative situations, functions, and topics

Van Ek, J. A., and L. G. Alexander. 1976. *The Threshold Level for Modern Language Learning in Schools.* London: Longman.

This book is now out of print but is a valuable compendium of grammatical structures, notions, functions, topics, and situations.

Tasks

Nunan, D. 1989 *Designing Tasks for the Communicative Classroom.* Cambridge: Cambridge University Press.

Pages 37–45 provide examples and rationale for "real-world" and "pedagogic tasks," Chapter 3, "Task Components" discusses the development of tasks in terms of goals, input, and activity types.

Prabhu, N. S. 1987. *Second Language Pedagogy.* Oxford: Oxford University Press.

This book reports on the Bangalore Project and the "procedural syllabus" developed there. Chapter 2 outlines 'pre-task' and 'task' with examples; Chapter 3 provides a definition of three types of meaning-focused tasks: information-gap, reasoning-gap, and opinion-gap.

Culture

Kramsch, C. 1993. *Context and Culture in Language Teaching.* Oxford: Oxford University Press.

This book provides an analysis of the complexity of the relationship between culture and context in the language classroom. Chapter 3 describes and analyzes five case studies of foreign language teachers teaching a class.

Brick, J. 1991. *China: A Handbook in Intercultural Communication.* Sydney, Australia: National Centre for English Language Teaching and Research.

This book is the first in a series of handbooks for ESL teachers. Although this particular book is about China, the exercises provide a model for how to work on awareness, attitude, knowledge, and skills in the area of understanding one's own culture as well as others.

Content-based instruction

Brinton D. M., M. A. Snow, and M. B. Wesche. 1989. *Content-based Second Language Instruction.* Cambridge, Mass.: Newbury House.

Provides rationale for and examples of sheltered, adjunct, and theme-based models. Pages 38–39 feature an example of a module on drugs, integrating topic, text, exercise type, language strategy, study and discussion skills, and notion and function. Pages 62–63 provide an example of a psychology course syllabus integrating reading, writing, study skills, and grammar.

Snow, M. A., M. Met, and F. Genesee. 1989. A conceptual framework for the integration of language and content in second/foreign language instruction. *TESOL Quarterly,* 23: 201–217.

This article outlines the principles underlying the integration of language and content. It provides a framework for and examples of content-obligatory and content-compatible language teaching.

Strategies

Ellis, G., and B. Sinclair. 1990. *Learning to Learn English: A Course in Learner Training.* Cambridge: Cambridge University Press.

> Provides an introduction to developing and building strategies in the areas of vocabulary development, grammar, listening, speaking, reading and writing.

O'Malley, J. M., and A. U. Chamot. 1990. *Learning Strategies in Second Language Acquisition.* New York: Cambridge University Press.

> Provides a theoretical foundation for learning strategies with extensive taxonomies. Chapter 7 "Learning Strategies: Models and Materials," introduces their cognitive academic language learning approach (CALLA) model for integrating content, language, and strategies for elementary and secondary school learners. This chapter also examines materials for adult learners.

Participatory processes

Auerbach, E., and N. Wallerstein. 1987. *ESL for Action: Problem Posing at Work.* Reading, Mass.: Addison-Wesley

> The activities in this textbook exemplify the principles of participatory processes.

Selecting and developing materials, activities, and techniques

Omaggio Hadley, A. C. 1993. *Teaching Language in Context.* Boston: Heinle and Heinle.

> Includes sections on strategies for teaching listening and reading comprehension, a curricular planning guide for teaching writing, and strategies for teaching culture.

Celce-Murcia, M., ed. 1991 *Teaching English as a Second or Foreign Language,* 2nd ed. Boston: Heinle and Heinle.

> Includes sections on teaching listening, speaking, reading, writing, grammar, and vocabulary, as well as chapters on planning lessons and textbook selection and evaluation.

Hutchinson, T., and A. Waters. 1987. *English for Specific Purposes: A Learning-Centered Approach.* Cambridge: Cambridge University Press.

Chapter 10, "Materials Design," provides a model for designing ESP materials and various examples of materials developed from the model.

Organization of content and activities

Dubin, F., and E. Olshtain. 1986. *Course Design: Developing Programs and Materials for Language Learning.* New York: Cambridge University Press.

Pages 51–63, provide examples of ways of organizing a syllabus.

Nunan, D. 1989. *Designing Tasks for the Communicative Classroom.* Cambridge: Cambridge University Press.

Chapter 6, "Sequencing and Integrating Tasks," offers principles of sequencing and integrating tasks with examples from published materials.

Soars, J., and L. Soars. 1986. *Headway Intermediate.* Oxford: Oxford University Press.

The table of contents of this intermediate-course book provides an outline of one way in which structure, usage, and vocabulary are integrated with the development of reading, speaking, listening, and writing skills.

Evaluation

Brown, J. D. 1989. Language program evaluation: A synthesis of existing possibilities. In R. K. Johnson, ed. *The Second Language Curriculum,* 222–243. Cambridge: Cambridge University Press.

As its title suggests, this chapter gives an overview of evaluation, what it is, its various purposes, and how it can be carried out.

Hughes, A. 1989. *Testing for Language Teachers.* Cambridge: Cambridge University Press.

This is a teacher-friendly, accessible overview of the types and purposes of testing and evaluation, with guidelines for constructing tests of the four skills, grammar, and vocabulary.

Nunan, D. 1988. *The Learner-Centred Curriculum.* Cambridge: Cambridge University Press.

Chapter 8, "Assessment and Evaluation," examines the relationship between assessment of student learning and evalution of the curriculum, and provides examples.

White, R. V. 1988. *The ELT Curriculum: Design Innovation and Management.* Oxford: Blackwell.

Pages 148–156 examine the formative role that evaluation plays in curriculum development and the ways in which teachers and learners can provide data for such evaluation.

Consideration of constraints and resources

Rodgers, T. S. 1989. Syllabus design, curriculum development, and polity determination. In R. K. Johnson, ed. *The Second Language Curriculum,* pp. 24–34. Cambridge: Cambridge University Press.

This chapter provides a useful checklist of constraints for use in planning curricula in "real time."

Index

Note: Page numbers followed by *n* indicate footnotes, *t* indicate table, and *f* indicate figures.